THE WANDERINGS OF A
WONDERING JEW

For Pat

His 'Fidelia', wife and mother of his three children
Allegra, Zuleika and Yehudi, who typed this manuscript
and loved him for the rest of his life.

THE WANDERINGS OF

A WONDERING JEW

by

CAMILLE RACHMIL HONIG

Bright Feathers Books

British Library Cataloguing in Publication Data
A catalogue record for this book is available from the British Library.

ISBN 978-1-8384806-0-8

Typeset by Amolibros, Milverton, Somerset
This book production has been managed by Amolibros
Printed and bound by T J Books Limited, Padstow, Cornwall. UK

List of Illustrations

CHAPTER ONE

I was a peculiar son of a Peculiar People. I was not even like other children of similar Jewish homes in Poland. First of all there was a whole to-do before I came into this world. Ardent prayers and tears and innumerable visits to holy men, to *tzadikim*, to miracle Rabbis in the provinces of Poland and Galicia, and of course to famous doctors and "Professors", both gentiles and Jews. I was expected to be born as if I were a prince destined to wear a crown and inherit a kingdom. Eighteen years had passed since my father and mother had married – and my mother was barren.

There was no greater misfortune for a Hassidic family of our class than to be childless; not to have a *Kadish*, that is for the son to say the prayers three times a day for a whole year after the death of a parent.

Father would rise, I was told by my grandmother, at midnight and sit on the floor with a candle at his side and shed bitter tears of the *Kh'tsos*, midnight prayers which Hassidic Jews perform every night except Friday evening, the beginning of the Sabbath. "You were prayed for as if you were the coming Messiah," said my grandmother Chana, wiping her eyes and blowing her nose.

This phrase was so often repeated to me in later years that I grew up almost with the idea that I have some connection, some mysterious affinity with the Messiah. I was expected and he was longed for; no wonder I developed very early a kind of Narcissism and I loved to speculate on the Messiah and, if it should turn out that I was not the Messiah, I must at least be the forerunner of the Redeemer.

Besides, I looked forward to the coming of the Messiah for less exalted reasons: There is a passage somewhere in the Talmud, our

Rabbi explained to us, that although we are now obliged to study the Torah and Talmud day by day (just as God does) – as if God doesn't know already! Didn't Moses write it word for word, including the Torah by word of mouth – (the Torah She'bal-peh) under His dictation?

But, explained the Rabbi, when the Messiah comes we shall cease learning the Torah, there will be no need to learn the Bible (mistakenly translated as the *Law* in the New Testament), and live by the Torah of the heart – in the words of Jeremiah – and we shall all be perfect. Now this I thought was an excellent idea and I was grateful to the rabbinical mind who invented it. For the truth to tell we were desperately bored by most of the holy Torah and the Talmud. We were badly taught the Bible and we missed the grandeur and sublime poetry of the Prophets.

We learned by rote, the Rabbi translating into Yiddish and we children repeating it in a special sing-song. And the same with the Talmud which had quite different melodies, Oriental, Moorish, Arabic; a kind of chanting that is as old as the hills and stems probably from the eleventh century Spain. Of course we loved a great deal of the Bible, the wonderful stories of Moses, Joshua and David – Abraham, Adam and Eve and, although we were quite puzzled by the irascibility of Jehova – whose exalted name we were never allowed to pronounce – who made such a fuss and got so angry with Adam and Eve over an apple – that nothing less than expulsion from Paradise would do and with all the consequent miseries that were to befall them and the human species as a result. Frankly, to my childish mind, I thought the story unfair and plain silly.

That was about the beginning of my "Bible Criticism" at the age of five or six.

As to the Talmud, I liked the Agadah more than the Mishna and Gemarah, which seemed to me plainly boring and of no interest to a young boy.

Then I heard from the Rabbi another bit of good news about the coming of the Messiah: There is somewhere in the Talmud a story that one secret part of the pig we will be allowed to eat in the fullness of time, but *which* part will be revealed to us when the Messiah comes!

Hurrah for the Messiah! Not that I wanted or craved at that time to taste such an abomination as pork, *Chazer* (the very word made me sick) but somewhere deep in my heart I had a secret longing to see what it tasted like and to see if I would survive such a monstrous sin.

So the idea that when the Messiah comes he will reveal to us which part of the pig we may eat was an alluring thought, and the abolition of this sin by the grace of the Redeemer, was a fascinating idea.

Several years had to pass until I actually had the "abomination" in my mouth, and lo and behold – I couldn't swallow it and had to spit it out. And this happened on the holiest day of *Yom Kippur*, the awesome fast and prayer day when every Jew, man and woman from the age of thirteen is not allowed to swallow even a mouthful of water. On that *Yom Kippur* day I went with a colleague, a boy called Abram, to the river *Pilica* beyond the dark woods of our little town Tomaszow. It was a lovely autumn day, and we went through one of the finest residential streets, where at the corner was a Polish butcher shop with a handsome display in the window of various sausages, hams, and a delicious looking white piece of meat, which I had never seen before. The whole window looked like the still-life of a Flemish painting.

I asked the woman at the marble counter for a half a pound of "that white stuff", pointing to the window, the name of which I didn't know. She cut off a piece with a sharp knife as it if were a piece of cheese, weighed it and wrapped it up.

My colleague waited outside the shop to look out for Jewish passers-by. We made our way to the woods where we sat down, took out the rolls and butter from our pockets, unwrapped the parcel and started the forbidden feast with this most tabu of meats.

We started eating, first a bite of roll and butter and then a piece of that white stuff, which we cut up with a little pocket knife, and looked at each other to see who is going to be struck down first by lightening – or God – for breaking His law. Nothing happened. Only we couldn't swallow the stuff – it made me sick and I spat it out. My friend did the same: "This isn't ham at all, this is raw (*Speck*) and needs to be cooked first," he said, and spat out his mouthful too. Obviously he had eaten ham before – I didn't know the difference. It must have been lard!

The Bible is right. Pork is uneatable, I thought. I had a brilliant idea of going into a peasant hut to see whether I cannot persuade the peasant woman to give us milk in exchange for the pork. She looked a bit suspiciously at us but gave us two glasses of fresh milk, still slightly warm from the cow, and I gave her the uneatable "uncleanliness". We drunk it there and then and finished off the rolls in the woods – and slowly recovered from the shock of the abomination.

Although I no longer feared God and I was not afraid that he will strike me down right there and then, I was, on the other hand, deeply disappointed in what the *goyim* eat. Is this what I had been so hankering after? No wonder Moses had forbidden it! It was truly disgusting, and I was convinced that I had had in my mouth a piece of ham.

As to God – I was no more afraid of Him, for some two or three years before, I had a deep quarrel with Him, so serious that I wasn't even on speaking terms with Him. I ceased to pray to Him. At this time I was barely eleven years old when something happened to me which was the most tragic and horrifying experiences, bound to impress itself on a child of that age for his whole life.

It happened on a Friday winter evening when I returned with my father from a Synagogue after the evening prayers. I was a little disobedient, and he was annoyed with my behaviour. I don't remember exactly what I had done but he had given me a very slight slap on my face, which I resented, and I was sulking. I wasn't saying a word to him and my small cold hand in his warm hand lay unresponding. The dirty snow was lying in the street, the cloudy sky was dark with a few stars only and half a yellowish moon.

Our dining-room, which opened into the kitchen, was well lit with a gas lamp; a pleasant warmth came from the white tiled stove, and a delicious smell of food, of gefilte fish and chicken soup, and stewed pears with cloves, sugar and vinegar hit our nostrils.

"Good Shabes," said my father to my mother – and I repeated it after him by way of a greeting. Then father took off his heavy overcoat and walked up and down the dining-room, chanting joyfully the traditional "Sholem Aleichem" in honour of the angels who are supposed to accompany us from the house of prayer to our homes.

There were supposed to be three angels guarding us – and not only us but every Jew who comes from the Synagogue on Friday evening. They were invisible.

Father washed his hands at the bowl, and so did I, reciting a short prayer. After which he went up to the table laid with four silver candlesticks with lighted white candles, a decanter of home-made raisin wine, silver goblets, and two loaves of white wheat bread made with eggs covered with a silken cloth, on which there was stitched the Hebrew words *L'eKovet Shabes* ... for the *Honour of the Sabbath*.

Father would say, and I after him, Kiddush with a special melody, the blessing of the Sabbath wine. Taking first a sip from the goblet he would hand it to Mother and Mother would give it to the servant girl in the kitchen. I would drink from my own small goblet. Then father, still standing, would uncover the white loaves taking up one, holding it to his breast and, first making a curve round the bread as if taking its measure and apologizing, he would cut four slices from the delicious *Chala* sprinkled with poppy seed, and each one of us would dip our slice in the salt-cellar and again say the traditional short blessing which is always said when you start eating a piece of bread: Blessed art Thou Adonai our God, King of the world, Who has brought forth bread from the earth.

This was a sacred ceremony because many a time, mother would say, that bread is a hallowed thing and if you drop it on the floor you must pick it up and kiss it. Father admonished me one day for thrusting my knife into the bread to cut off a piece: This is not the way! Only goyim, gentiles, stab their bread.

Father, on this evening, was using the new big bread knife which he bought in Warsaw, inset with mother-of-pearl and with letters in silver, the Hebrew word *LeKoved Shabbes, In Honour of the Sabbath*. He then covered the knife with a napkin, for a knife must never be left uncovered.

Father and I wore our black silk gabardines, and of course we had on our completely changed linen and fresh white shirts without ties, and black velvet round hats. Father had taken me with him in the afternoon to the local Jewish ritual baths, the *Mikve*, where he was lashed with a bunch of reeds in the hot steam baths on the highest steps, where the steam is thickest and hottest, after which he took a bath which was especially filled with hot water in which we both dipped ourselves three times. On Wednesdays the *Mikve* was used by women only. As in most towns, there was no such baths for Christians, except in the Capital. A Jewish town without a *Mikve* was as unthinkable as a town without a Synagogue. But only Jews went to the ritual bath, Christians – never. That's why it was said that a Russian or Polish peasant had only two baths in his life; when he is born – and when he dies!

Malka's mother, a cousin, an orphan, who was being brought up in our house, helped in the kitchen. She brought in first the gefilte fish, usually carp with its delicious jellied sauce, which had to be cooked early in the morning or the night before. Of all nights I liked Thursday nights best for mother got up before father, at about four or five o'clock, to prepare for the Sabbath and bake the *Chalas*, the delicate egg breads and to prepare the *tcholent*, a traditional speciality of fat meat with potatoes and barley, which was sent to the local baker on Friday mornings, cooked for 24 hours in an iron pot in the oven, and was brought back on Saturday by our maid in time for the midday meal. Each housewife made her own special sign on the pot so as to recognize it. Inside the big iron pot there was usually a smaller earthenware dish covered with a piece of clean linen. This was the famous Jewish *Kugel* – or pudding – of which there were several varieties, more or less like a Jewish Christmas pudding (if one may so designate a typically Jewish medieval dish) sometimes made with lokchen (a kind of egg spaghetti), dried fruit and chicken fat with spices. There was also another dish called *tzimes*, mostly carrots and raisins with bits of chicken fat and sugar. To finish off the Sabbath meal there was compote of stewed prunes, sometimes with apples, sometimes without.

All this huge meal was baked at the bakers ovens and prepared on Friday after the bread baking, for in no Jewish house must there be lit a fire on Sabbath, unless you have a gentile to make it. Such fires were allowed to be lit by a gentile servant on a winter Saturday, when they were called in to extinguish the candles or turn off the gas lights, for which our caretaker or his daughter received a special big piece of chala, or a drink of vodka.

Kozarek was the name of our caretaker who lived on the top floor and he had a wife, three daughters and a young son, whose name was Balek. Every Saturday Kozarek would come home and beat his wife mercilessly. He was drunk and the beating was usually done with a flail when he came home from his work in the granary. I once saw his handsome black haired daughter, Zosia, with large breasts, getting hold of his flail and giving her father a wallop with the heavy wooden rounded sticks, so furiously that he fell half conscious – half dead – to the floor, and the shrieks of "old Boga" and "zyowry" – son of a whore – could be heard at the bottom of the house. We never heard of such beatings in a Jewish house or home.

The younger daughter, Stefa, with thick blond hair and big blue eyes, who was our part-time servant, would run up the stairs when she heard the screams, shouting: "I'll kill that son of a whore! By God I will make a corpse of him if he won't let mother alone!"

He didn't dare beat up his daughters because they beat him back without mercy. Stefa would come down again to our kitchen shouting: "Next time I'll give it to him with an axe; let the cholera take him."

Stefa spoke Yiddish beautifully and I had no chance to learn Polish at that early age. She would even keep an eye on me and wouldn't let me take food before I said my morning prayers and washed my hands: "And what about *davenen*?" she would say, holding her arms akimbo.

Father sat at the top of the table laid with a white damask cloth, and shining with silver, in his black silken gabardine and his round black velvet cap, the traditional Sabbath dress, and I was dressed in miniature cloths like him.

After the Kiddish he and I washed our hands in the ceremonial way, first pouring water from a pitcher on the left hand and then on the right, using no soap. Father said the short benediction – the *hamotza*. After the gefilte fish, in the delicious jelly we dipped our chalas and then father would take a small glass of vodka, which he explained once to me, must be drunk by grown-ups not because of drunkenness but for the sake of not eating meat after fish, which is supposed to be "unhealthy", and a little glass of spirit – which he called "okevit" or aquavita – or simply "bronfen", would divide the two foods. After this we were served the hot chicken soup with the different varieties of lokchen, which were called shilgerlech, and with sugar beans or kreplach – pastry with chopped meat or liver, and kneidlech, for the last days of the Passover holidays.

Father would then sing in his low, pleasant voice, a traditional song in which I helped him in a weak voice in the "Zmiris", which I hardly understood.

There were medieval Jewish folk poetry in praise of the Sabbath *Malkusa*, the Queen of the Sabbath. Nobody who hasn't lived in a small Jewish town in Poland or Russia can have the slightest idea what the Sabbath meant to us. It was the whole transformation of the inner and outer life. Every Jew was a prince and every Jewish woman a princess. Isn't it written in the Holy Books that on the Holy Sabbath every Jew and Jewess gets an additional soul to his own? The poet Heine long ago wrote a poem about the Jew who is transformed every Sabbath as if by a miracle, from a despised, wandering "schnorer" into a prince. And isn't it said by one of our sages that: More than the Jews kept the Sabbath – the Sabbath kept the Jewish people.

After the *Zmiris*, Father would ask me what I have learnt during the week. I would fetch the heavy volume of the Talmud from the whole set of twenty thick volumes that stood in the bookcase, and he would examine me as to whether I understood the meaning and could translate in a special sing-song, the Hebrew or Aramaic into our Yiddish. To me the melody of the Talmud, the Gemarah nigum, was more exciting than the literal meaning of the words, which were often incomprehensible as the discussions and intricate sophistries of the Rabbis were dark, mysterious, and often plain boring to a child of seven or eight, which was when we started to study the Mishna and Gemarah, which comprises the whole Talmud with the commentaries of the medieval Rabbi Shlomo Ibzchaki, known popularly by his initials RASHI, the most beloved and gentle Rabbi amongst the commentators, and the discussions by the so called Toskpot, the descendants, German and French medieval Rabbis, who are very legalistic, abstruse, tedious and incomprehensible for a child's mind.

I remember still the particular book which I rehearsed with him, it was the volume *Psochim*, which begins with the ingenious problem: What is the position of the Law when one steals from a thief? … I

8

looked at the clock on the wall, I remember – it was ten minutes past six o'clock. The windows have been black for a long time.

Our great-grandmother, Lipke, my father's grandmother, who was then staying with us, and was over a hundred years old, but with her eyesight and hearing unimpaired, was in the kitchen. My cousin had run out for a while to a neighbour's house and had left the door unlocked. I was sitting facing the door, and after a few minutes I saw two men enter. They had black handkerchiefs over their faces and were dressed in ordinary suits and town hats. They rushed into our room. They had two small revolvers in their hands.

Father got up, holding a towel in his hand, in a defying gesture. He tried to fight them off, but they overpowered him, and I thought they pointed the revolver at the top of the big brown cupboard on the wall … But they had shot at him. He fell without a cry, without uttering a sound, on the threshold of the kitchen with his body in the dining-room. I ran into mother's room, where she was standing by the white stove, warming her back. I heard her plead with them: If you want money I'll give it to you – but they answered only: "Quiet, quiet, Cicho, cicho," and ran out through the door.

Mother ran after them screaming and I after her into the snow-covered courtyard.

CHAPTER TWO

The bandits escaped into the back streets. Mother and I ran back into the house and I saw father's head lying on the floor, his cheek with a tiny hole, a round bloody wound in his temple with a trickle of blood on the floor. His face was serene, his black eyes closed, and his grey-black beard undisturbed. I felt him with my hands, thinking he had just fainted. I didn't know what death was, never having seen a dead person.

Neighbours and passers-by, having heard the screams of my mother, came running in, and I remember opening the book of psalms which was on the table, and I began to pray from the Psalm book.

We had then quite a lot of money in the house, and I saw it being wrapped up in paper, perhaps several thousand marks, but hidden at the top of the big dark wall mirror. The bandits had taken nothing. The only thing missing was the big silver knife with the encrusted mother-of-pearl handle. The room was full of people, and I stood at the table praying for father's "resurrection".

I remember it so well because this was the last time I prayed to God with such urgent devotion and faith. Surely God would not allow such a good and pious man as my father to be killed like a dog? For I believed then and believe now that my father was one of the most generous men I have seen. Perhaps, at this time, I didn't yet know what a good-hearted man he was, having had no means of comparing him with other people. About his piety I was convinced, but probably only vaguely did I realise what a really good man he was.

German police came with a doctor. The doctor just slightly lifted his head and examined his temple with the small, bloody round hole.

He laid the head back. The police started pushing the onlookers back into the street. Everybody had to leave and mother, weeping, and I horror-struck with incomprehension, were taken over to my aunt who lived a few houses down the road. My great grandmother and my cousin were taken in by neighbours. Mother was lying on the bed wringing her hands and crying bitterly. I was lying near her, no longer able to cry but with a growing feeling in my belly as if someone had hit me hard.

The room at my aunt's house was filled with neighbours and strangers who, shocked as they were with the tragedy, were, nevertheless inquiring whether my father was killed because he was a Jew or whether this is perhaps the beginning of a pogrom of the whole town. The word Pogrom was an ominous and terrible word for me. I'd heard it a thousand times. But we didn't hear about pogroms when the Germans occupied Poland. On the contrary, strange as it may seem now, the German army was looked upon by the Jewish population as deliverers from the Russians, who were masters of pogroms.

And I well remember some two years before, at the beginning of the War, when the first German cavalry entered our town on magnificent horses and in splendid uniforms with fur caps on their heads (with the *"Torden H'tte"*) and with drawn shining swords. Riding in front amidst the officers and generals I thought that the German Kaiser Wilhelm himself was the leader of the Cavalry. Where else would a king be if not at the head of his army? Hadn't I read in the Bible how Saul and David fought with their armies?

The military police ordered everybody out and locked up the house and sealed the doors with red sealing wax. And there – in the locked house – they left my father in the dark.

There in my aunt's house, I was lying on the bed near my weeping mother, trembling as if a sudden cold had gripped my inside, a terrible painful sensation that I had never felt before.

What would happen if my father should wake up in the dark and find himself locked up? Oh – surely he would open the window and jump out! It was on the ground floor. Surely God wont let him die? And with these trembling thoughts I must have fallen asleep.

On the next morning, the Sabbath, the Black Sabbath, my mother took me by the hand and we walked over to our house where the military police had already arrived with an ambulance and taken my father to the mortuary, covered in a white blanket.

So it's true. My father is dead. I could not reconcile myself to this horrible fact, and I was for some reason ashamed, ashamed for God and ashamed of the shaking heads and tearful faces of our neighbours living in our street, as we passed to our house. The poor widow, the poor orphan, who was born after so many years of prayer to my father who, over night had become a Kodesh, a holy man, a martyr.

Who could have done such a crime? Who could want to murder such a good man? Such a tzadik as Reb Eli?

Who could have done such horrible evil to a man who has done nobody any harm, but only good to so many people? Why do this to such a righteous man?

Uncles, aunts, cousins, my grandmother and my great grandmother and neighbours came with us to the house. They could not comfort my mother because my father's body was still lying as we had left him the night before.

Then came questions. Why him? Nobody else was killed, nothing was stolen, there was no pogrom in the town. Then somebody remembered that a few years ago a whole Jewish family, father, mother and three children had been murdered by Poles with an axe in the middle of the night; Only one little girl whom I knew, Toblia, about eight or ten years old, had escaped with wounds; they thought she was dead. Apparently my father had been the first on the scene of the massacre, their house being a little further up the street from ours. And father had been a witness in the Court. This was some two or three years before and I remembered well the tragedy. One of the suspects was a Pole called Novak. He had a hare-lip and small straw-coloured moustache. He had threatened my father's life in front of witnesses. I had seen him once or twice in the street since then and I was terrified of him. I was, since I can remember, since my childhood, terror-stricken of the stories I heard at home and in the Cheder of pogroms by Russians and Poles on Jewish towns and villages. Murderers and robbers where a constant terror at night, and sleeping with Father in the same bed, I would tremble with fright when I heard him snoring. I remember a few years back that I heard of such a robbery. Thieves broke in through the back door, just outside the wall of our bed-room, and stole a big earthen jar, like a barrel, full of jewels and gold and silver, which my mother took from people as security when she lent them money without interest (father refused to take things in pawn). Mother even accused him that if she'd let him he would give away everything – and leave his wife and only child to starve! My mother, I thought, was not such a generous person as father, as I had many times observed. I saw him, for instance, giving money to his poor friends, Chassidim from the same *shtibel*, so that they could go into our shop, where mother was in charge, and pay her for the groceries they "bought" from her for the *Mlave Malke*, Farewell of the Queen of the Sabbath, the evening meal, which is, amongst the Chassidim, eaten in the company of other Jews. Or my father would bring home an "orech" a guest for the Sabbath meals, usually a poor, homeless Jew who went from town to town collecting charity for his family or for a dowry for his daughter, or simply for himself. They were wandering Jews, simple folk unversed in the Torah and Talumd, but often great scholars and pious Jews. Many were wandering Rabbis from small towns who had some written commentaries on the Holy Bible, or pious sermons often quite worthless rubbish, but they aspired to fame and honour, but found no publishers, so they collected "subscriptions" or subscribers whom they promised to have their names printed in the usual lists on the last pages of the book of the recording of the names of the Jews with their towns, if they made a donation to the worthy cause, which will assure them a place in the *Gan Eden*, the Paradise in the "World to Come". Father would glance through such a manuscript, read a passage here and there, or a page, and if he found anything worthwhile he would put in the book a ten ruble or a twenty-five ruble note, and give it back to the scholar, and give him a few other names of well-known or well-to-do Jews who would like to get a "piece" of *Olam Habah*, in the World to Come at a bargain price. The wandering Jew would go away murmuring blessings for a long life, *naches* from children and good health and happiness.

It was these kind of Jews that he liked to bring home on Friday evenings, or on the Sabbath for a meal, and very often I would wake up in the morning and find in my bed such a stranger with a long beard, who would ask: "What's your name, Yingele, and do you know a Shtikl Gemorah?" But some were common Jews of doubtful character, who could hardly say or read a prayer in Hebrew, commonly called in Hebrew *Am Haarerz*, an ignorant man from the land or a peasant. Others were rogues and adventurers or thieves, and you had to watch the silver or table linen or it would disappear. Some were gentle people with melancholy eyes and handsome, scholarly faces with well combed beards, and you could see that they had known better days or had come from good homes and, although their gabardines were worn and their shoes down-at-heel, one could see that they were not schnorers, common beggars, but that they were simply "Yordim" – fallen Jews.

There was quite a variety of these schnorers, some genuine victims or refugees from the provinces or villages were there were pogroms, others whose businesses had gone bankrupt, or their homes had burnt down, or other misfortunes. Most of them had no trade and were permanently unemployed. Others who were poor because his father-in-law had, for one reason or another, stopped supporting them. Many were Yeshiva *bocherim*, or Talmudic academy youths, did nothing but sit all day long in the Synagogue studying the Talmud and "ate days" – that is, went every day to another Jewish home to have their meals and, when they married they "*ate Kest*", or had board and lodging at the father-in-law's house; sometimes for as long as eight to ten years, a duty which was undertaken by the father-in-law at the signing of the marriage agreement in addition to the dowry which was usually given to every daughter, depending on the riches or poverty of the bride's parents. *Madan*, or dowry, was one of the oldest Jewish and oriental customs, and unfortunate was the family who couldn't provide a dowry for his daughter. So great was this mitzvah – good deed – that a special communal fund was set up and, even among the poor homes, there were special boxes for "*Hachnoses Kale*" – bringing in the bride – together with boxes for the various charities, like hospitals, Talmud Torahs, schools for poor children together with the famous Talmudic saint, known and loved in the Jewish world as Rabbi Meier Baal Haness the miracle worker, which went for charities in Palestine.

As to the charities for the Holy Land, there were very many of them; since time immemorial dozens of people used to appear from nowhere as delegates or Meshulochim, messengers from Palestine, collecting money for all sorts of causes; hospitals, yeshivas, Talmudic schools, widows, orphans and the homeless – without end. They came in various types; modest, honest with thin spiritual faces and mystical eyes, and clean kempt beards, dressed in modest coats or gabardines with Rabbinical fur caps or Shtramuls. Others were fleshy, vulgar, insolent, with phoney letters of introduction from some unknown charitable society or some obscure Rabbi. Father would give to all of them, in addition to the local charities, or the many poor towns people and professional shnorrers or beggars who would go twice weekly from house to house, from shop to shop on Tuesdays and Fridays, and again some would stand meekly at the door and accept gratefully, with a thousand blessings, even if pieces of sugar or bread were given. Others would ask insolently: "Is that all?" Or he or she, for many were women with children in rags (often not even their own) and would argue: "I cough with blood and this is all I get!" – and would throw back the bread or even money, insolently and with curses. One of the Sabbath *Orchim* whom father invited to the Sabbath, a man with a comically long nose and red beard, who travelled for a society for dowries for brides in Jerusalem, told us a story which made us all laugh: He met once a Catholic priest who asked him with a good-natured smile: "I know that Jews are a charitable people, I understand that you collect money for widows, orphans, hospitals, schools, old-age homes, the poor, the sick, but I cannot understand the fuss you make about collecting money for bride's dowries?" I answered the priest very simply, I said: "You see, some two thousand years ago we failed to collect money for a young Jewish woman – and look what happened? We have been suffering for it ever since!"

That tragic Friday evening there were no "guests" at the table. Had my father brought home somebody from the Synagogue he too might have been shot, and mother and I too might have been killed.

It was nothing but a miracle, said the neighbours, recollecting the mass murder of a whole family of five people. That evening I also invented the first big lie of my life. When I was asked what I could remember of the murder, to which I alone was the witness and might have been killed with him as I was nearest the gunman with the mask, I invented a story that I saw one of the suspects, the man with the hare-lip about whom I had heard that he had threatened revenge on my father on the occasion of the murder my father had witnessed. I also lied that I tried to protect father when he was lying on the floor, saying that at that moment when I threw myself on him I had pushed off the paper mask from the man with the gun whilst I was trying to push him away. This was a pure lie and though, inwardly I was terrified at the macabre scene I was witnessing, I was nevertheless, with my invented heroism of trying to save father, making myself appear less cowardly than I actually was.

The whole thing was untrue, because actually father was standing and facing the bandits and I was standing by his side, petrified with terror, looked straight at the gun in his hand, and his mask was on his face.

This lie has worried me for a very long time and, when I was interrogated by the German police investigator, and the man with the hare-lip, Novak, was brought before me, I said that I recognised him. As I was a minor this identification was considered as insufficient evidence. But I was pleased with my assumed role as a "protector" of my father and acclaimed for my heroism with admiration, although I was only eleven years old.

Chapter Three

That Friday evening changed my whole life and was the strongest and most tragic event that formed my character. That trauma which struck me so suddenly was to last for a life time, and I naturally grew up as a neurotic boy, inclined to depressions and anxieties.

A day later was the funeral. The whole town of Jews, and even gentiles came to follow the bier which was carried by four people and which was covered in black cloth. I was taken by my uncle's big hand, and it seemed to me that I was carried on the waves of a black sea of mourners. After the men, came the women with covered heads with my mother. Their screams and wringing of their hands, so characteristic for Oriental mourners, were heard down the streets, and all the shops were closed in the streets. Some women, especially the poor who had received alms from father, tore their hair and cried in a traditional sing-song, and they wailed in penetrating mourning voices. The praises of my father's goodness of heart, his generosity, and his great piety. Some women screamed to God: How could he allow such a crime on so saintly a man? And which Jew will be the next to be murdered?

At the grave to which I was led, I repeated after my uncle, the Kadish prayer, which is said in Aramaic by a son in mourning for his parent. I looked down into the grave, where father was laid in his white linen garments, the "*soives*" and Tales, and on his closed eyes they put two broken pieces of shards.

One of the Rabbis, who had first given the funeral oration at the Synagogue, stood by me and put his hand on my head. I don't remember crying, I felt only an unspeakable terror, and at the same time I was aware that I was being looked at by the whole congregation as the centre of attention, if not as the chief mourner with my mother, and my alleged "heroism" of trying to save my father from the murderer.

There was another macabre touch to the burial when a small barrel of blood had to be buried with him: This was because it had been ordered by the police that there had to be a post-mortem, which has a sinister sound in Yiddish – "palmesan", an operation which is forbidden by an old religious Jewish law as a desecration of a corps. And as blood is considered sacred, the blood had to be buried with him – even where father fell on the floor and a trickle of blood from his wound was taken up and buried with him in his grave. The blood of a martyr which mustn't be desecrated.

The days that followed were a kind of living nightmare. Since I can remember I had suffered from bad dreams, now they became terrifying. I used to walk up and down in a sweat, shivering. I remember many falling dreams; I used to fall slowly from Heaven, from which some dark angels with dirty wings dropped me.

Once I remember I dreamt of a boat, suspended by four chains, which was dragged up to Heaven. I dreamed about the Messiah; a young, beautiful face; dressed in a medieval robe and hat; sometimes he would look like one of the poor, strange "guests" that father used to bring home; or the prophet Elijah, who, according to ancient legend, will precede the coming of the Messiah, and he will not be recognised by anyone. He, Elijah, may take on many disguises; he may look like a beggar, or a peasant, or a weaver (as my poor uncle was) although a pious man and a Talmudist. Sometimes I tried to discover whether the simple Jew might be one of the *Lamed Vovniks*, which, according to an ancient beautiful legend, are so holy that they go around in disguise as ordinary poor people, and whom nobody recognises, and they themselves don't know that they are saintly. There are thirty-seven *Tzadikim* (*Lamed Vov* is the number thirty-seven in Hebrew), for whose sake this wicked generation of sinners is not destroyed by God. Every generation has such thirty-seven *Lamed Vovniks*; without them the World could not exist for one day. And in my world of reality and in my dreams, I saw only such mysterious people and saints, who do not know themselves that they are saints – for, as a Chassidic Rabbi has said: "The man who knows he is a saint, is no saint!"

A different nightmare started when coming back from the grave-yard. At first mother and I had go to through two rows of people waiting for us, as the chief mourners, to comfort us with traditional words: May God comfort you amongst other mourners of Zion and Jerusalem. After which we travelled home in a drozhko with the hood up so that nobody could see mother, who had a black silk lace shawl thrown over her head, covering her grey, tear-blotched face and red eyes. My dominant feeling was of shame, although I was still engulfed in fear and indescribable pain, I was overcome by another feeling of abstruse shame. I was ashamed of all the uncles and aunts and cousins and the black mass of strangers and neighbours who pitied us and expressed with their sad looks and shaking of heads and wringing of hands over the poor orphan. I was ashamed of the clear blue, cold sky; I was ashamed of the trees; I was ashamed of Heaven and Earth: I was ashamed of God.

How could God allow such a murder of a good, pious man? Where were the angels that Friday night who accompanied us from the Synagogue to protect us? How could an almighty God, full of mercy and compassion, look upon such evil and allow the innocent and the righteous to suffer?

That father was a good man I knew, not only from the little experience I had of him myself, but everybody told me so: My mother, my two grandmothers, and my great grandmother: "You have a father, a tzadik", they would say, "and you ought to grow up like him and emulate him."

Now my grandmother Chana said that father, her beloved son, was no less than a *Kodik* (mispronouncing the word *Kodesh* – a holy martyr), who provided dowries for all her daughters, and he would be reckoned amongst the other Jewish martyrs who fell in the pogroms.

And, in addition to the same for God, there began to rise in me, secretly in my heart at first, a thought that frightened me more than anything else, that this might be the ultimate blasphemy against God;

suddenly, a thought which I knew was a mortal sin! At last – I am free of father and his God!

How can I be secretly glad that my father was dead? And yet I felt it deep in me, and I was glad and horrified at the idea – that now I am free – without a stifling authority either or father or God.

Though I had never felt the heavy hand of my father on me; he had never laid a finger on me, and when he sometimes spoke sharply to me, when I did something he disapproved of, or I didn't say my prayers properly; only once in my life, I remember, I ran away from him one evening, out into a dark side-street, he ran after me and I was terrified of him and wished he would fall and die. But this was only a momentary thought, which struck me like lightening, in a moment of childish rage and fear.

When we came home from the funeral the house was full of mourning; there were tiny stools on the floor. The big marble decked looking-glass, which stood by the wall was covered in a long white sheet as custom requires, and an aunt was handing us hard-boiled eggs with the skin off, dipped in ashes. We sat on these low stools or boxes, the beginning of *Shiva* – or seven days of mourning, during which time we were visited by family, neighbours and friends. The whole town of Jews came, and there was a *minion* or a quorum – of ten Jews especially for the evening prayers, after which I said the Kadish, reading from a prayer book as I didn't yet know it by heart. We lit a perpetual light – a *ner tomid*, a burning wick in a silver vessel, which burned for a whole year, day and night.

After this is was permitted for the people to comfort the mourners and praise the dead for their good deeds, piety, generosity and saintliness, with typical oriental exaggeration and tragic gestures. Tears must be in moderation, as you must comfort the bereaved. Before the funeral you mustn't comfort them, but after burial it is a *mitzvah* – a good deed.

The poor and the distant relatives were especially loud in their extravagant praises. One elderly woman lamented loudest and tore her hair, re-telling a story about the kindness and mercy of father who had run one night in a snow-storm to bring a doctor to her sick child, had paid the doctor himself and given her money for medicines.

And how he had brought a chicken and oranges (which was fruit – unimaginable luxury) for her child. A young, distant relation who lamented in a particular shriek, and tore her hair in despair, shouting her sorrow for all to hear, because they said that she expected money from father for her dowry. The men, among whom were some of the Chassidim of my father, the learned, the poor and the rich, sat on ordinary chairs (only the family sits on low stools) and quietly told each other prayers about the goodness of my father, and the innocent blood that was shed, and that is only the beginning: Other Jews, like him, the whole town, may be in jeopardy.

Reb Shmuel Yellin, a friend of my father, who had at the cemetery made a solemn tear with a pocket knife on the lapel of my black gabardine as a symbolic sign of mourning, and tearing one's clothes which is only done to the sons of the mourning family, said something about "the end of days", and "the steps of the Messiah", which are obviously approaching. Reb Shmuel, who used to chew the corner of his long gray-brownish beard and rub his forehead when he contemplated "the end of days", was a melancholy, poor Jew, a flour merchant, but a great Talmudist, with five children. He also wanted to know how long the Redeemer will be in coming to save His people. People still spoke of the persecution and pogroms in Russia and Poland. I almost learnt about the word "Pogrom" from the time when I started with difficulty learning to read a Yiddish newspaper. So I listened when others read it to me. Especially I remember listening to the notorious Bailis case just before the War. I remember the year, it was 1913, I was eight years old. We had heard for the last year or more these preposterous tales about Bailis, which we children, in Cheder (school) knew was an impossible, unbelievable, monstrous lie.

A simple, ordinary Russian Jew was made over night into a Jewish national hero and martyr – or arch-villain – and catapulted into world-wide fame. He was Mendel Bailis, a manager in a brick plant in Kiev, who was accused of having murdered a Russian boy, who was found killed in a bog. Bailis was accused of killing him in order to use his – "blood for making the Jewish Passover Matzot." It was a libel from the Middle Ages that Jews committed this ritual murder every Passover in order to take the blood of a Christian boy to make the Matzot. This libel was repeated almost every year in various countries, from Poland to Hungary, to Damascus, to England, from the middle ages. Grizzly tales were told about these supposed ritual murders and stabbings in Churches all over the world.

I must say that I despised the Christians for believing such unimaginable calumnies. Don't they know that Jews mustn't eat even *animal* blood? Don't they know that meat must be drained of every drop of blood, and must be kept in salt on a special draining-board, and soaked in water for at least an hour before cooking? Don't they know that mother used to send me dozens of times with fertile eggs, which had only a speck of blood, to give them to our Polish caretakers, because we mustn't eat them? And how many chickens or ducks, which were not ritually clean (not Kosher), because they had pimples or other blemishes on their intestines, did I take over to our Polish neighbours, because we mustn't eat them? Don't they know that the Bible says that blood is life, and human blood the most sacred?

And yet, for centuries, they have accused us of this blood libel, which we called in Hebrew *Alilas Dam*. For centuries and centuries, since the earliest middle ages, remembering that in the first Christian era, the Romans accused the Christian sects of murdering and eating their human sacrifices. And how Christians, who suffered from the same calumnies, now accuse the Jews of this crime. And in our own days of enlightenment this Bailis case should happen (infinitely worse than the Dreyfus case of which we heard so much, and in which one ordinary French Jewish officer was accused of spying for the Germans). But here was a far greater accusation against the whole Jewish people and it's religion.

Jews of the whole world were interested in this monstrous slander, and followed it with baited breath, when names like Prinaitis and Shmakow, for the prosecution, quoted the Talmud to prove that Jews must use Christian blood for their Passover Matzot. And the Defence of Gruzenberg and Chief Rabbi Mazoh, who proved that these are long discredited falsifications, which even Pope after Pope nailed as a lie.

One day, I remember, mother sent me to some neighbours down the road to get quite a large sum of money which she had lent the woman (who was called in town, for some mysterious reason – Aristotle – although her real name was Blumberg), I remember saying to her: "Mother asked me to get the money she lent you", and Aristotle answering: "Go home and tell your mother that Beilis has been freed – and that she doesn't need any money!" I did as I was told, and mother and father were overjoyed with the news.

For some time before the Christian children in our street would attack us and call out in derision: "Hey! Zydzic, Bailisic, Jew Bailis!" And we'd run away. But it so happened that this time there was a Polish Catholic Priest who was sent to prison having been accused of raping and murdering a Polish girl. The name of the priest was Macoch, whose notorious name was on every Jewish lip, and when the Polish boys called us Bailis, we called them in Polish: "*Bailis Zyje – a Macoch w kozie gnije!*" (Bailis lives, and Macoch rots in prison). Whether I was the author of this memorable rhyme or somebody else, I don't know or remember. It soon became very popular among the Jewish boys who clung to it as a defense against their detractors. After Bailis, Macoch's name came to us as a Godsend.

Chapter Four

We slowly recovered from this nightmare and then, in the summer of 1914, war broke out. We were convinced that after all the persecutions and pogroms in Russia and Poland the Messiah must come, and when finally the war came we saw in it nothing less than the war of Gog and Magog, which is the forerunner of the coming of the Redeemer.

The Redeemer came, ironic as it may seem, in the guise of the German army that, within days occupied Poland.

Our small town, Tomaszow, on the river Pilica, was for a time the front line of the German-Russian battles, and it changed hands several times. I remember the fear of pogroms when the Russian army was in occupation; the heavy bombardment of the *Dicke Berta*, the "fat Berta", Germany's most terrible weapon, and the big guns which we saw moving with heavy artillery into the town. One day the huge wooden bridge which divided our town into two was blown up and the bang was so great that I thought the whole town shook as if in an earthquake. We wondered at the miracle that we were still alive and our houses were still standing. Our house was littered with machine gun bullets. Some Russian solders hid in our basement and the Germans came in and drove them out. When the Russian army entered the town there was fear everywhere, and while the army marched through the streets, followed by heavy guns and private and military cars and army vehicles, groups of soldiers under the leadership of sergeants came into our shop and to many other shops, demanding money, vodka and food. They took out with them sack loads of stolen provisions and money.

When this war was going on for some days, even when our shop was closed, father begged a Russian officer to do something about the open robberies which were led by Local Poles as well as the passing Russian soldiers. The Officer, a man with a kind and handsome face, immediately put two Russian solders on guard on the steps of our shops, who stood there and guarded our lives and our goods for hours until the Russian army had passed. I looked at this handsome officer with a little brown beard, and believed what mother said that he must be a guardian angel, or perhaps the prophet Elijah in disguise, sent specially by providence to guard our lives and property.

After Russia and Poland, Germany and Austria were even civilized countries, where the Jew, if not loved was at least respected. Emancipation of the Jews, the forerunners of which were the French Revolution and the armies of Napoleon, came to Germany just after post-revolutionary France with the Rights of Man, and Napoleon's so-called Synhedrion Germany, since the great days of Mendelssohn, towards the second half of the eighteenth century, was the dream land of every young Polish and Russian Jew. To emigrate to Germany, to study at a German University, was the secret desire of every Jew. We had a name for those Jews: They were called in Yiddish, *Daitschen* (German), to wear a short European suit and black bowler hat was to be dressed like a Daitsch. To speak Yiddish with a German accent was to speak *Daitschmerish*, and as Yiddish, the people's language of the majority of Eastern Jewry, was a close relative to middle high German, with many Hebrew and Slav elements, it was called Yiddish-Taitsch, and to its detractors it was merely "Jargon." It was brought to Eastern countries by German Jewish immigrants who developed this language in the late middle ages, and within a short period of a few hundred years, created an original literature of its own, and in particular, in the last hundred years, produced remarkable Yiddish writers, some of great originality like Mendele, Sholem Aleichem, Peretz and Sholem Asch. Through them we reached the German Jewish enlightenment of the Mendelssohn period, and the great German writers like Lessing, Goethe, Schiller, Heine, who were to be found in many Jewish homes. It was reasonably easy to understand the German language with Yiddish as a background.

Modern Jewish history came first to us from Germany; the first great modern Jewish historian, Heinrich Graetz, was the most popular historian and was read in Yiddish translation and in German.

The first books I ever bought was a set of ten volumes of Graetz, bound in brown leather, which I had, however, been forced to return because such advanced free-thinkers books were thought to be dangerous and might lead us astray and away from the orthodox path!

I was beginning to doubt the Bible story and the Talmudic theories that God created the world only for the sake of the Jews. On the other hand I was pleased to discover that the Talmud affirms that there are righteous Gentiles in the world, and that they are entitled to an honourable place in the "world to come", together with righteous Jews.

I was afraid of the goyim, not only from what I heard of the bloody persecutions and slaughters in the past, in the far off Middle Ages during the Crusades and the Inquisition in Spain, but I was afraid of the Polish boys who threw stones and mud at us, and made fun of our long coats, round little black hats and the peculiar earlocks, which children of the Chassidic sect had to wear. At the same time I was jealous, and envied, the Christian boys their freedom; they were allowed to go bare-footed in the winter and in the summer. That some of them were so poor they didn't have any money to buy shoes or warm clothes didn't occur to me. I envied Balek, our caretaker's son, who was sometimes my playmate, his complete freedom. Not only did he run about with his long, straw-coloured hair and without earlocks, but without shoes – in rain – or even snow.

I wanted to try a bit of his sausage or ham, which he sometimes took out from his pocket and eat with a chunk of black bread, but I was afraid it will make me sick, or I will die on the spot for eating this forbidden food. My nights were full of fears and nightmares; I was afraid of ghosts, evil spirits, Shaidim and Mazikim, witches of Satan himself; and fallen angels, and dybukim, who entered into your soul and made you sin.

I was afraid of barking dogs at night, a sure sign that the angels of death were abroad – the Malach Hamoves. I was afraid that I will see my shadow in the moonlight without a head – which will be the end of me. But I was afraid above all of the burning fires of Hell in the world to come, in spite of the assurance of the Rabbi that Hell doesn't work on the Sabbath, and in order to get used to burning in the fires of Hell, I would prepare myself by getting used to burning by holding my hand over a lighted candle or an oil lamp or a coal fire. (I was very careful to see that I shouldn't burn my hands severely!) – so sure was I that I am destined to go to Hell for the innumerable sins that I committed. I was sure that I had even caused the death of a neighbour's innocent child of about two years old, for the sheer fascination I had with black magic and occult knowledge; This is how it happened: I must have been seven or eight years old, deeply impressed with the uncanny stories that my grandmother, Chana, who was as full of medieval superstition as a pomegranate is with seeds, had told me: She said that it is a well known belief that if you open a child's eyes while it is asleep – it will surely die! One Summer afternoon when I was alone at this neighbour's house and saw the child who was fast asleep in a cot, it was a little girl whose father was a house painter, and who also painted outrageous and frightening portraits of people that I knew, but could hardly recognise – for they looked like goats or bats or lizards, foxes and asses. When he left me alone in the room with the sleeping child, I was suddenly overtaken by the "Evil One", who made me go to the cot and find out for myself if its true that children die when you open their eyes whilst they are asleep. Trembling with fright, I braved myself and carefully opened first one eye – and then the other. The child slept on without a sound, and woke up later for her bottle. Nothing had happened!

But imagine how I felt when, a week or so later, I heard that the child, a little girl, had died! She had been ill for only two days, and here was I, the murderer who was responsible for her death! Surely, it must be true what grandmother said to me that she is afraid that my soul will not enter even a *frog*, and that I will have to be born again and again, and pass all seven stages of Hell! And I told not a soul of my secret crime.

It must have been shortly after this that, having discovered my mysterious powers, I began to develop into something of a shaman – or miracle worker – to impress my young school friends. As my ideals changed suddenly from being the Messiah and accepted a somewhat humbler destiny as being a General of my own army, which I fed with stolen huge boxes of chocolates, or supported with kopecks, also stolen from my father and mother; I became an expert thief. I was particularly on the look out for silver coins which father suddenly found in his pocket on the late afternoon of a Friday, before the beginning of the Sabbath when all Jews have to empty their pockets of any money which happened to be there, and we left it in various hiding places, in cupboards, under the table oil-cloths. I already began to "desecrate" the Sabbath by handling this money and, out of sheer challenge to the Almighty, to touch candlesticks, candles, pen and pencils – and such like things which are forbidden on the Sabbath. And whenever I could I would break the law of not waiting six hours to eat milky food after eating meat – and two hours between eating milk before meat. I knew I was sinning, but the challenge excited me. Our lives were so bound with taboos and "Don't" commandments, as for instance, not to run on Sabbath, not even to walk longer than a very short distance, and not to carry anything in one's pockets, not even a handkerchief. But if you *must* carry a handkerchief, you should bind it round your neck, when the handkerchief becomes automatically a piece of apparel. We were suffocating under the Rabbinical Laws which bound our lives. We envied the Polish boys their freedom. They didn't have to worry about washing hands in the morning after you get out of bed, and saying prayers, and only afterwards to be allowed to have breakfast. The prayers were endless, three times a day, late afternoon and evening, and a special prayer – Krias Shmah – before going to sleep. We were constantly under God's watchful eye. And then, all day till eight at night, in the Cheder, the Jewish school, which hadn't changed since the medieval times, Summer and Winter. When snow was falling inches deep, or there was a bitter frost and the windows were covered in frosty fantastic designs of flowers; Father would sometimes carry me on his shoulders, wrapped up in a sheep-skin and a round fur cap – or bashlik – with high boots and galoshes.

Our Cheder, the like of which you can still see in Arab countries and in Muslim India where they teach in the same method the Koran, consisted of one large room which served as kitchen, dining-room and bedroom. There was one dim window, so frozen over in winter that you couldn't see out of it or open it even in the summer. There was a table, and a bench on which we sat while we were repeating the Holy texts of the Bible and the Yiddish translations of the Rabbi.

Our Rabbi, Itzchik Milter, was a little man with a short grey silken beard and earlocks. He very often used to put slices of horseradish on his forehead as a sovereign remedy against headaches and migraine, from which he suffered: It draws out the pain, he said. In the corner by the stove sat a mongol little woman with a huge swollen head like a pumpkin, who uttered shrill noises whenever the boys used to throw pieces of bread or fruit at her. We were so used to that monster that we didn't mind her at all, neither were we frightened by her moronic behaviour. She was the Rabbi's misbegotten daughter whose name, or age, nobody knew.

We sat, if we were not called to the table, on the floor, and played all sorts of games.

One day a little boy of about six or seven, whose little penis two older boys had tied up with cotton until it was blue, screamed with pain and the Rabbi had to cut the tied cotton with scissors. Every child got a thrashing, except me – as I was a privileged boy of a well-to-do father. I never even got my hand smacked. One day, when we started to learn the Talmud, I put down my head on my hand as if I had fallen asleep. The Rabbi called my name when my turn came, and a boy said that I had fallen asleep. Don't wake him, said the Rabbi. From then onwards I made quite a habit of "falling asleep" while learning a difficult and boring page of the Gemarah. We were in this airless, dingy Cheder from early morning till the evening. At about twelve o'clock our maid would bring me something to eat – a roll and butter, a hard-boiled egg and an apple or pear and a glass of milk, which I either shared with someone or often gave away to a hungry boy. The Rabbi pointed with an ivory pointer across the lines of the Bible or prayer-book, as we laboriously pronounced the words in Hebrew or Aramaic, which were quite difficult to read for a young boy. I used to have special difficulties in reading and a special teacher had to come to me at home, three times a week.

The earliest years of our youth was spent in such a medieval, depressing school without having the opportunity to go out and see fields with corn, or a forest with trees. Nature didn't exist for us – we knew not the names of flowers, except the rose because it is mentioned in the Bible.

When I was truanting from school, I usually ran to the sand-dunes at the outskirts of the town, where I played soldiers, I naturally, being the General. I had a little sword and got hold of a second-hand pair of binoculars. We used to attack on the big hills of the sand-dunes, my army and I. We were always doing well, as a Roman General would report. We had heard from the Talmud about the Roman Generals, Emperors and brutal soldiers. We learnt of the destruction of Jerusalem and of the atrocities on our people and the Holy Temple, the Beis Hamikdosh. We knew nothing about the Romans, or the Roman Empire – we only knew Vespasian and Titus his son whose legions raised Jerusalem to the ground. We heard of Hadrian who suppressed the rebellion of the Bar-Kochbah. We heard of other Jewish heros, Bar Giora and Gish Chalov, who were carried to Rome with other Jewish notables and fighters. All this seemed to have happened only last year. For did we not fast and sit on the floor of the Synagogue every year on the right day of the month of a beery Summer to mourn the destruction of Jerusalem?

Ah! If only I had been a General then! I would have killed Titus, the wicked ha-Rashah, as young David killed Goliath. I deeply regretted that I wasn't there when Titus shed so much blood. I would have shown him! But I had heard that now there are also great generals they were called Hindenbeg and Ludendorf, the German generals who defeated the mighty Russian armies in battle after battle in East Prussia, and almost at our door in Tomaszow and the River Pilica. They didn't murder Jews, on the contrary, they protected us from the Russian armies. And we heard that when the Germans entered Warsaw, there appeared posters on the walls and houses, addressed to the Jewish population in Yiddish and German: *Zu meinen lieben Juden* – and signed, "General Ludendorf". We admired Germans and hoped they will beat the Russians and free us from the pogrom nightmare.

We, being of the "rich" families, didn't suffer hunger, but the black bread we eat was half sand, and the salt was black. Under the Germans we had little food, unless you got smuggled meat and butter from other towns or villages. There was no sugar, and we had to have our tea or coffee with pieces of boiled sweets or awful tasting saccharine; sometimes we would use honey as a sweetener in tea.

The Germans were very "orderly" and correct – not like the Russians. The German army confiscated – requisitioned – the Russian – robbed!

One day, I remember, father bought up a large consignment of skins of oxen and calves and horses, all folded in squares and covered in thick, rough, salt for preservation. There were several huge cart loads of these smelly, black and brown skins, and a group of peasants put them all, one by one, in a big deep disused well, that stood in our courtyard. Father never dealt in such merchandise but a Polish landowner and farmer sold it to him – "because there is bound to be a shortage of leather."

Within less than a week, a German officer with a group of soldiers, looking for hidden metal, found this big well, whose stinking smell gave it away, and they dragged out all the skins from the well and drove them away in lorries. Father was taken with them in a car and, as he told it later, the Commandant treated him politely and gave him a special receipt to be paid for by the Kaiser after the war.

Not long after there came out a military order that all articles of copper steel and brass had to be delivered to the Commandant, and everybody had to take off even the brass door handles and window locks, which were exchanged for rough iron handles. Although it was a great nuisance and the requisitioned articles a great hardship – we didn't mind as much as we did the Russian army's sequestrations and open robberies. The Germans did it to the whole population – the Russians robbed first of all the Jews, and we considered ourselves lucky if there was no pogrom, and people were not beaten up and killed.

All our sympathies were on the German side, and we rejoiced when the German army of Hindenburg destroyed the Eastern front and freed city after city from the Russian hordes. The Germans were looked upon as the bringers of civilization. Russia and Russian occupied Poland was a poverty stricken oppressive and wretched prison. We still remembered the "Cantonists", Jewish boys of the age of 8 to 10 years, forced into the Russian army and made to serve for 25 years in remote parts of the country or in Siberia. "Nikolayewsky" Soldiers they were called, and it was no better than being forced into hard labour. We remembered the pogroms and the expulsions from the villages into overcrowded towns where the poverty was soul destroying. We also remembered the Bailis blood libel which had made our lives into Hell. It was impossible for a Jew to live in St. Petersburg and Moscow unless he was a Pierwoguildy Kupiec – or Merchant of the First Class.

When one Saturday a whole army of Cossacks entered on their magnificent horses, followed by an army of slant-eyed Kalmuks on their small horses which looked like ponies, we thought our city was doomed. Fortunately the commanding officer was a man with liberal ideas, and he promised the notables of the town who went to beg for help, that there will be no pogroms on Jews so long as he is alive. And I remember that Sabbath night when we were all already in bed, a loud knocking at the front door, and when father let in several Kossacks with tall sheepskin hats that almost touched the ceiling, coming to see if they cannot find any sleeping quarters, when they saw that there was not enough room in our small house, they left without saying a word. We looked upon it as a miracle. When a day or two later, in the midst of a severe Winter, a Russian Army arrived from the East, people said the Russians brought with them the terrible frost of Siberia. The whole town had that strong, most pleasant, smell of the boots of the Russian soldiers, a smell of the famous French perfume Cuir de Russie, which I discovered years later in Paris, and which became my favourite that brought back memories of childhood. Fear and trembling disappeared, and the pungent smell of Russian leather remained with me as a delicious memory for ever.

The Russians didn't stay long and retreated within a week or so. There was a heavy battle, and we could hear the heavy cannonade, and see the blazing fires across the bridge. The Poles were on the side of the Russians. We were waiting for the German army. The front changed hands several times near our town and forests, and I remember that our Polish caretaker, Kozarek, threatened father to "Wait till *ours* will come!" ("Clekaj az nasi przyda!") – *OURS* meant the Russian Army.

Chapter Five

In the neighbouring town, Ujazoc, Polish hooligans denounced several Jews as German spies because they could speak to Germans in Yiddish, which was closely related to the German language, and two Jews were actually hanged as "spies".

We heard of the great victory of the German Army, lead by the enormously moustached Field Marshal Hindenburg who broke the Russian armies at Tannenberg.

About the battle on the Western Front we heard very little, but we knew that England and France were fighting the Germans. We didn't know where England was, and when I first looked at the map of Europe, England looked a small Island on top of the world in the corner of Europe, but exactly where it was – nobody seemed to know. France too was a remote country, and what we knew about it was that its Capital, Paris, was the most wicked city in the world, where women danced almost naked with black stockings, and sang lewd songs, and drank champagne. We particularly thought of this famous City as the City of the falsely accused Jewish Captain Dreyfus, who was finally freed and cleared of all charges brought against him.

And from my aunt I heard, when I said I would like to go to Paris, that the City is the most dangerous one in the world, and as an example she told of her own fiancé who broke off his engagement to her, went to Paris, married a French woman who, one fine day – poisoned him with arsenic!

Although we knew less about England, we heard that the Jews there were free, and that a Jew, Disraeli, was the Prime Minister; and another Jew, Moses Montefiore, was very rich and helped Jews everywhere by building schools, hospitals and colonies in Palestine, and that the Czar asked him for a loan of millions of roubles. Although he died years ago before I was born, he was still a living legend with us, and many stories were told about his piety and his philanthropy; that he prays three times a day and keeps the Sabbath so Holy, that he wouldn't open a letter – not *even* from the Queen!

There was a story going around which I didn't fully appreciate at the time: A poor Jewish woman in our small town asked: "Who is this Jew, Montefiore, about whom I have heard so much?" She was told about his immense riches – a second Rothschild – and that he is a pious Jew who gives charity to Jews and Gentiles alike. She asked further – where he lives, and when told in London, she asks where London is: In England. And where is England? So she is told that England is about two weeks journey by horses, railroad and boat. And the woman sighs and says: "Poor man, what has he with all his riches, when he lives so far away from any human habitation!"

It was not at all amazing that we knew nothing about England. We never saw an Englishman. We never heard English spoken, whereas French was the language of European culture, and we often heard French words and phrases broken into a speech by the intelligentsia, and one of the commonest praises about a girl was to say: "She speaks French and plays the piano." At schools only French and German were taught as foreign languages, never English.

For the Jews in particular Germany was not only our neighbour but the dreamland of our future, where religious and cultural emancipation began.

Germany was the longed for country, and the youth escaping from the Russian and Polish ghettos were flowing into the Swiss and German universities, just as the poorer classes, workers and craftsmen were longing to go to America.

The War was not to us between Germany and England, but between Germany and Czarist Russia, and we hated Czarist Russia and the Czar and his oppression, his persecutions, his corruption, with its government-organized pogroms by the *Czarna Sotnia* (the Black Hundred), who were responsible for massacres in dozens of cities, from Kiev to Gomel – to Warsaw and Kishenev.

And Brusilov's Armies were defeated by Hindenburg and Ludendorf. We were overjoyed. And yet there were hundreds of Jews serving in the Russian army, who had to shoot at Jews in the German army. Stories went round of a Jewish Russian soldier shouting to a German soldier: "Don't shoot! Don't you see that people are running," and some often, so we were told, shouted to each other the ancient Jewish credo *Shemah Israel*.

But we knew nothing about England and less about the British Empire, which nobody seemed to know where it was. Yes, of course we heard that it was a free democratic land with the oldest parliament in the world, and where the Jews live in freedom and prosperity, but we couldn't understand how such an enlightened country as England who made it possible for a Jew to become a Prime Minister, could ally itself with that backward, oppressive and pogrom-ridden Russia, who still organised ritual murder trials, as we had seen only recently before our own eyes in the Bailis trial of the blood libel.

So we prayed for a German victory over the forces of the "black hundred". Suddenly one day we heard the unbelievable news that the Czar was forced to abdicate, and with it the whole Czarist cruel regime with its armies came tumbling down.

We heard about Kerenski, the Democratic leader, which brought hopes for our future. Then we began to hear about the second revolution and such leaders as Lenin and Trotski, who overthrew Kerenski and formed a Soviet, which promised the people bread and peace.

By the time of the treaty of Brest-Litovsk I could already, with some difficulty, read the Yiddish newspapers that came from Warsaw a day late. We were not a little proud that Trotski and Yaffe were the leaders of the Russian delegation, and peace between Germany and Russia was signed. Our lives became a little more secure and free from Russian pogroms.

The local Synagogue politicians now spoke significantly about an American President called Wilson, who had announced his fourteen points for peace, and assured everybody that the promised peace is soon to come.

Meanwhile as the Germans withdrew from the Eastern Front, we saw Polish riders on horses and our town's doctor, Narewski, in old Polish uniforms, riding through the streets and disarming German soldiers, who willingly gave up their rifles and guns and even their short daggers without the slightest struggle.

Poland had gained Independence. Free again from the oppressions of Russia, the Polish Government in Warsaw proclaimed the Republic of Poland. Jews rejoiced – but at the same time were apprehensive.

What will happen now? Will there be pogroms, or, as they were officially called in the papers, "excesses" or "disturbances?" There were. And a number of towns suffered casualties in killed and maimed, and Jewish houses were looted.

But worse news came from the Civil War in Russia which soon broke, and reports came that thousands of Jews were killed by the White Armies. And that the only protectors of the Jews were the Red Army. Particularly bloody, we read in the papers, were the pogroms in the White Armies of Petlura, Koltchak, Denikin and the Ukraine.

Then, when Europe was still celebrating the Peace, the newly resurrected Poland was at War with Bolshevik Russia, and Polish armies under Pilsudski were marching on Kiev.

The propaganda and hatred against the Bolshevik Government was not only directed against Russia, but mainly against the Polish Jews – who were the leaders – as everybody knows, of the Russian revolution, and that this was all part of the plot by International Jewry to take over the World!

One morning, going out from our house, I saw huge posters in glaring colours on the gates of our courtyard, taking up nearly half of the space. On it was a caricature of Trotski, his face and hairy body pink, as if the fires of Hell were shining on him, his huge black eyes with a long Jewish cracked nose on which were his famous pince-nez, and his little goatee beard. He was holding a smoking gun in one hand, and a dagger dripping with blood in the other, and sitting on a mound of skulls with rivulets of blood flowing from underneath, and burning churches and towns in the background. Across these posters was the slogan: "*If you don't want him to enslave Poland – FIGHT.*"

These posters, and they were plastered all over the town, made us afraid to look at them. They boded no good, and we were expecting a pogrom by the passing Polish Army. There was panic in town, and people began a whispering campaign that many have packed their bundles and all they could carry and left for the bigger cities, Warsaw and Lodz. Stories were told of Rabbis and notables shot as Bolshevik spies.

These posters were harbingers of massacres and destruction of Jewish homes. The town was in the grip of terror. But as if by a miracle – nothing happened, except for a few Jews getting beaten up.

The Russian Bolshevik armies were marching on Warsaw, we were expecting them any day. Then the miracle happened: the "*cod nad wisla*" (the miracle on the river Vistula), and the Russian huge Army was beaten by the Poles.

Now everybody said our turn will come, because the whole populace was told that the Russian Revolution was made and is led by Jews. So Poland's next duty was to get rid of the Jews. Jewish faces darkened when they saw the ubiquitous propaganda in the press, posters and leaflets about the Jewish menace. And soon we heard that the Polish army under General Haller (called Hallerczyki) let their boys have a go at the Jews in Poznan the district and other towns.

Life became a nightmare, Jews were thrown out of running trains, their beards torn out, their small businesses ruined and there were bloody pogroms in many towns.

It was a year or two after the great event of the Balfour Declaration in which England solemnly promised a Jewish National Home in Palestine, when Warsaw streets were plastered with posters: Zydy do Palestiny (Yids to Palestine) and Poles were called upon to boycott Jewish shops. Life became uncertain and we were afraid of what the morning will bring.

Some of my friends did go to Palestine, others went abroad to Berlin, Paris, Brussels.

"What is he whose grief bears such an emphasis? Whose phrase of sorrow conjures the wandering stars and makes them stand like wonder-wounded hearers?"

HAMLET

It was now that another tragedy shook me. My mother, whom I loved a little more than my father, re-married a man with three children. I looked upon this marriage as a betrayal of my father. I was not taken to the marriage ceremony in the house of a relative, but a cousin came to me with a piece of cake which I couldn't eat and threw away.

Next morning, when I went home from my aunt's place, I remember feeling a terrible shame when I walked through the street and people were looking at me. I felt that everyone was feeling sorry for me, and blamed my mother for her marriage so soon after the murder of my father. I was ashamed to look people in the face, as if my mother had committed open adultery.

My step-father turned out to be a decent, harmless man who had lost his fortune sometime ago when he became a widower. But I hated him (for no other reason than that he married my mother) and his two daughters, the younger a very beautiful girl, and the boy a little younger than I. I called my mother "Mimishi" (Little aunt). And it seemed to me that I had lost all my mother's love. I fell into an undisguised melancholy. I suffered from terrible dreams; from a repeating nightmare of falling like a wounded angel with broken wings. I was falling head downwards into an unfathomable abyss. I was no longer the forerunner of the promised Messiah, but an abandoned, betrayed child of a Jew who had been killed in front of my eyes – and even his mother had betrayed him and his father.

And again, as when my father was murdered, my disbelief and I began my prayers with derision, suddenly I disbelieved in God made me ask unanswerable questions – which millions of children must have asked before – If God created the World – who created God? I found no answer and none of my play-mates and fellow school children had any answers. Some said that they never thought of such a question. My friend Moishe who went with me to the Talmud-Cheder, which was a higher school than the Torah or Bible school, and where we learnt also German and Polish, giving up very early the Russian which we learnt at the beginning of the War, my friend Moishe, who was the son of a Talmudic scholar and a pious Jew, said that such questions are forbidden to be asked and that it is a mortal sin even to contemplate them. All these answers, he said, will be given when the Messiah will come.

But I, secretly in my heart, no longer believed in the Messiah, but this ultimate apostasy I was afraid to utter. I loved the Messiah as I loved my father, and all of a sudden I lost both so tragically.

CHAPTER SIX

I was twelve years, and I had become a fully responsible Jew a year earlier than the proscribed 13 years, when one becomes a Bar Mitzva, and started to put on the phylacteries every morning, except on the Sabbath and on the Holy days. I went every morning and evening to the Synagogue to say Kadish after my father three times a day. I felt a little more important than the other boys – who were not orphans and said no Kadish – and, as the months went by, I began to lose faith in the words of prayer by which I was supposed to open for him the Gates of Paradise. I no longer believed in the Aramaic words of praise and the *Isgadal Ve'Iskadesh Shemai Raba*, with which the prayer begins: Hallowed be the great name – sounded hollow, even a mockery – when the "Great Name" has allowed such a senseless murder. There is probably nothing there, and the Heavens are empty; only the graves are full with the dead.

An unobserved heresy straight from the Book of Psalms struck me very early: "The dead cannot praise Thee, neither those who go underground."

There were days when I began to miss the Kadish in the evening, and I just didn't go to the local Synagogue where I was spied upon by relatives and neighbours, but went to town for a walk over the bridge. An uncle, a corn and wheat merchant, whom I didn't like, and who was a fanatical, rigid and ignorant man, took on himself the duty of being my moral guardian. He was a torment to me with his fanatical bigotry, and I despised his ignorance and his severity. He didn't know a word of the Talmud, and I felt insulted when he told me how to say the prayers or read the Bible, whose literal meaning he didn't comprehend. He was, perhaps, not a bad man, but as he had no children of his own he took it on himself to take my father's place in the eyes of the family.

His wife (my father's younger sister to whom he had given a dowry and paid for the marriage feast), my aunt Lea, was a simple naïve woman who didn't understand the world and thought that the "end is nigh." She thought that the Messiah is coming any day; the dead will rise from the grave and will roll themselves underground to the Holy Land in a general "T'chiyas Hamaisim." She believed that my father was a saint and sits now in a special place reserved for *Tzadikim* (saintly Jews). She believed that when the Messiah will come, the Jews will pass over a bridge made of paper, and the wicked goyim will go over an iron bridge – but the Jews will pass safely and the wicked goyim will be drowned in the rising stormy seas. I too will walk over a paper bridge to the land of Israel. She took great care of me, and loved me as if I were her own son. She gave me money for special delicacies, and cooked for me delicious meals – the most delicious you could think of. Her husband, Moishe Aaron she hated because he was mean to me, and she would give him the left-overs from my meals. At least once a week she said she is going with him to the Rabbi to get a divorce. The noisy rows, screams and bickerings went on for days and weeks. I shut myself in my room and didn't take any notice of it – I got so used to it – although from my father and mother I had never heard an impolite word spoken between them.

Aunt Lea was a good woman, and must have been a comely woman when she was young, but she neglected herself terribly out of hatred to her husband. Because I was the son of her beloved brother and she had no children of her own she lavished on me all her care and love. She thought that I am destined to become a great Rabbi as the son of a martyr and Tzadik, who was born because the Holy Rabbis had promised my father a son. She told me that father had been advised to let a Sefer Torah – a scroll of the Bible – be written by a special scribe. To have a special Holy scroll which is written on dozens of rolls of parchment and then sewn together, is a great Mitzva, and good deed, which is written in the book of life and death. The writing takes several years, for the scrolls are written in an ancient calligraphic script which hasn't changed for some two and a half thousand years. The lettering of such a Torah or Pentateuch is written slowly, word for word by a very clean and very pious man, whose sole livelihood this is, and is called a *Sofer*. He usually writes it at home or in the house of the donor. There were such pious scribes who, before writing the Tetragramaton Yaveh, (which no religious Jew ever pronounces, but substitutes it with such words as Hashem – The Name – or Adonai), would first go to a ritual bath, the Mikve, or to the river and dip themselves three times. And there were those who even went to the river when it was frozen in winter, and broke the ice with a hammer and submerge themselves in the icy water. How they did it I have never been able to understand – the miracle is that they survived.

After this they go back and write the Holy ineffable name. I used to watch the scribe in our house where he was sitting in seclusion and undisturbed in a separate room by a big table, so that he could spread the parchment, and write with a goose quill (no other pen is allowed) with a kind of Chinese black ink, which left a bold script with a permanent lustre. He would sit all day, after the morning prayers and breakfast, and he was nourished only by glasses of hot tea and lemon to which he would suck a sugar cube which mother or our maid brought to him.

I was fascinated watching him dip slowly his quill in the silver ink-stand, and murmuring slowly the Holy words of the Torah, word by word, as he would write them down like an artist in perfect calligraphy. He was so completely immersed in his holy labour that he sometimes didn't notice when I came in, or when he was brought a glass of tea. But sometimes he would raise his dark melancholy deep-set eyes, in face that was covered with a wide grey beard, and say to me: "You see, all this is for your sake because your father made a vow that if he will have a Kadish, he will let a Sefer Torah be written. You ought to grow up a good Jew and bring joy to your parents and your people.

When the Torah Scroll has been finished there is usually a public feast and rejoicing, like a Holy wedding. Mother meanwhile did the woman's work and embroidered a beautiful red velvet cover, with golden thread, with the name of my father and my mother which is put on the Scroll together with the silver ornaments, as if it were a crown on the Torah. I remember the finishing, "Siyem", when the "*whole town*" – that is all the Jews – were invited, the rich and respectable and scholarly Chassidim were invited, together with all the poor and ordinary beggars. I must have been about five years old for I remember the tables covered with white linen, and enormous quantities of herring, gefilte fish, and plates of chicken and goose. I remember the white carafes of vodka and red Hungarian wine, of which father used to keep in the cellar in several small barrels.

The womenfolk kept in the background, laughed and blessed me, and wiped their tears and their noses. Father and several people I didn't know, poured the wine in glasses; a few provincial Jewish players formed an "orchestra", which usually consisted of a violinist, a flute, a bass and a trombone with a drum. They used to play on Jewish and Christian weddings, and the "Porutz's" (noblemen's) Ball. The rest of the week they were selling fish or poultry in the market places. Some of the world's great violinists in Russia came from such players. My first Beethoven and Schubert I heard from such an orchestra.

The Scroll, attired in it's velvet cover with the golden embroidery, and with it's little silver bells, silver crown and ornament plate, was then carried through the packed streets, followed by a joyful crowd of men and women, dancing, laughing and wishing each other happiness and *naches*.

The musicians went in front of the procession, mother was behind with her neighbours, sisters and friends in the separate women's crowd.

I was with my father, who held the Torah in his arm close to his breast, and me by the other hand, as if the Torah and I were of the same holiness. Old Jews and young were actually dancing in the streets, and holding each other arms, stretched out on their shoulders in the manner of Chassidic ecstasy.

The Polish neighbours stood and gaped on the pavement in bewilderment, and good-naturedly shook their heads: The Jews have gone mad and are performing their black magic. People shouted "Mazeltov" – good luck – as if my father had had another son. Then the Torah was carried to the Synagogue, where it was put in the Oren, the Holy Ark, where, together with the other Torahs, it stood and was taken out only on Sabbath and Mondays and Thursdays, and every week a chapter was read from it. I felt immensely proud of the Ceremony, and it reminded me of a wedding of a cousin of mine that I had seen some time before, when the Torah like the veiled bride was brought under the white canopy under the stars. Only a child who has been brought up in such a home can realize the holiness of a Torah Scroll.

There are printed Bibles in the Original in practically every Jewish home, but the Torah Scroll is not kept at home but in the Synagogue, and it is a special honour to be called up to the Torah to hear a chapter read by a special Baal Koreh, the community's reader. Originally every man called to the Torah from the congregation was supposed to read the chapter for himself, but in order not the shame the unlearned Jews, who could not read the difficult Holy text, the Rabbis ordered that a special reader was to be appointed in every Synagogue. For not every Jew who can read the printed Bible can also read the manuscript Torah, which is quite different, and is often difficult to pronounce the words of the Hebrew which are written without vowels.

No other object is so holy in the Jewish ceremonial as the Scroll when it is carried to the reading table from the Ark. Young and old rise and kiss it, either directly by kissing the velvet cover, or by touching it with his fingers wrapped round in his Talis – the prayers shawl – which he wears, and then he kisses the prayer shawl. Thus I was initiated into the mystery of the Torah, about which Jewish history and legend is full of the most marvellous tales.

It is the Holiest book in Jewry. It was written by Moses under the dictation of God himself. Many saints have died a martyr's death, or were burnt with the Scrolls of the Torah, and the letters of the Torah fly up right to Heaven. And blessed is he who can afford to have such a parchment Bible written and presented to the Synagogue for the glory of the Holy Name.

It was no wonder that the son of such a pious and generous man as my father, should grow up to do great deeds for his people. And I sincerely began to believe that I am not just an ordinary boy of Chassidic home, but the One perhaps to be the forerunner of the Messiah.

I prepared myself secretly for the part by acting out various mysteries, or Kabbalistics ceremonies, about which I read as soon as I had mastered, for me, the formidable art of reading miraculous tales of Chassidim. Of these I liked best the stories about the Baal Shem Tov (The man of the Good Name). The Baal Shem Tov I knew from stories that my father and my Rabbis had told me. The Baal Shem Tov, I much later discovered, was born over two hundred years ago in a small village Mizbizh (Meidzyboiz), in Russia. To me he seemed a contemporary. He revived Chassidism, a sect that has survived until our times, and you can find them from Golders Green to Israel, and from Stoke Newington to Brooklyn.

The Chassidim, the pious ones, are now a new sect; there were Chassidim at the time of Jesus.

But the Chassidim that the Baal Shem Tov brought to life were a version of religiosity quite new to Jewish life.

Perhaps, if one looks for an example among Christian saints, one could find no better Chassid than the Tzadik Francis of Assisi. In him was the love of all God's creatures, there was absolute goodness and humility. There was the holiness of nature, of trees and flowers, of rivers and mountains, of the bounty of the fields, of wheat and corn, of fruit and vegetables, which God has created for man. The Baal Shem was a seemingly very simple minded Jew. It was said by his brother-in-law that he was not a good Talmudist, but before he was to reveal himself, not until his thirty-sixth year, he was a poor obscure Jew, who made a living by being an assistant teacher (a belfer) of a Melamed, and he used to take children on his shoulders and conduct them to school. Then he earned his bread by going with his wife to the nearby Karpaty Mountain, and dug out clay into a hand-cart which he dragged to the village and sold it for a few kopecs of gulden. He was also a ritual slaughterer, and was dressed like a butcher in a short peasant coat, to hide his real identity, for to be a "nister" (a hidden Tzadik) is the first step on the road to saintliness.

Sometimes these tzadiks go through life as one of the Lamet Vov Tzakim (the thirty-seven righteous men) who hold the world together. It was only through his disciples, known as the great magid, the wandering preacher of Mezzitch, who saw his face enveloped in a blue light, that his fame spread all over the land. Then the most miraculous stories began to spread and were finally spread and collected by one of his disciples, Reb Jacov Josef whose book in both Hebrew and Yiddish we all read. We heard stories from our Rabbis and wandering preachers about other great Chaddisik Rabbis, the Shpoler Zaide, that the grandfather of Shpole, the saintly Shmelke of Nikolsburg Zishe of Hampal, and many others, down to our own days, in faraway Bohemia beyond the mountains. As soon as I was given a little money, I eagerly awaited the travelling book salesman, who arrived with a sack of Bibles and other religious books and Chassidic stories, bound in paper covers, which I used to buy from the vendors who put up their stores at the exit door of the House of Study. He would also sell prayer shawls, prayer short garments and prayer books bound in cedar wood of the Holy Land; new shining Phylacteries (which one could not wear before Bar Mitzwa – that is until one is thirteen years old).

Every month I bought many such books, as well as cheap novelettes, which my father frowned upon. Sometimes I would exchange several old books for one new one. Most of the stories were about the miraculous doings and wise sayings of the Rabbis; about their holiness, charity and devotion, which they preached, and which warmed the hearts and fired the imagination of young and old. I believed all the miracles that were told about the Tzadikim. When such a Rabbi passed, my father would take me to this holy man to be blessed, to grow up to study "the Torah, to marriage and to good deeds."

Some of these Rabbis lived holy lives, some were ascetic and fasted every Monday and Thursday. Others fasted from Sabbath to Sabbath (for it is not permitted to fast on the Sabbath). As a boy I once visited a Rabbi, whose name I forget, who, I was told, fasted forty years from Sabbath to Sabbath, with the exception of Holy days. It was said that he was fasting so long because he was the son of a common tailor, instead of being the son of a Rabbi, and he became a dynastic Rabbi, as most of the later Chassidic Rabbis were. It was enough to be a brother or a grandson of a Tzadik. When this inheriting of the Rabbinical chair became the practice, it was actually the decay of the great Chassidic Movement, and some were so rich that they travelled like monarchs, and held "Courts" to which Chassidim would come and visit with donations and gifts.

The fasting Rabbi I saw, when I was about eight years old, has left on me an extraordinary, marvellous and frightening impression. I can see him now, as I entered with a donation in my pocket, sitting in a darkened room with closed shutters, and the Rabbi was dressed in a huge fur coat and a wide fur hat, sitting at a small table and looking into a book. I couldn't understand the fur coat he was wearing, because it was such a hot mid-summer day. He had a very long, light brown beard, streaked with grey, and his eyes were so deep set, his face boney and long, and his skin was the colour of a yellow candle.

Famous Rabbis used also to stay with us, and father entertained many travelling magidim. But at least once a year, he travelled to his own Rabbi, whose Chassid he was, the Rabbi of Skierniewice, a little town, not far from Warsaw.

Once Father took me when I was not older than nine or ten years old. The Rabbi was sitting alone at a long table, several books and a big volume of the Talmud was opened on the table, with a red handkerchief on it. The Rabbi made an immense impression on me; I was overcome by the sheer dignity and beauty of his person. He was very tall and his *straimel* (the large fur hat) made him still taller. His broad and very long beard covered his whole face, so that only the nose and eyes, under black eyebrows and a white forehead, were visible.

It is the custom of every Chassid to bring a donation – a *pedron* – to his Tzadik, or a present. Father put down a sum of money under one of the books, and I presented the Rabbi with a present of a crystal jar, mounted with silver, and in it was a pound of Russian tea. Father also put down a little piece of paper, on which was written his and his mother's name, as well as my mother's name and mine, also the particular request that he wished to make. This was called a *quitel*, which reminded the Rabbi to pray for you and give you his blessing. This was traditionally written in the entrance hall where the Rabbi's Shames usually wrote and received a little present of money. In this quitel it was written and especially mentioned that I was plagued by bad dreams and night-terrors.

The Rabbi looked at the piece of folded paper, told father and me not to be afraid of these night terrors, and assured me that the angels, Raphael and Michael will, from now on, be guarding me in my sleep, only that I must say my prayers properly and, in particular, the shema before going to bed. I promised, and he gave me a little pinch on the cheek and blessed me. He also gave me an ancient silver coin, which I should put round my neck in a little linen bag and wear it always. I wore the little bag on a cord round my neck, under my shirt. At first I thought that the horrible nightmares had left me for ever. But very soon they returned – but I didn't tell anybody. The last time I remember when father took me to the Rabbi was on the anniversary of the Yahrtzeit of the Rabbi's father, the famous Tzadik of Qorki, a town near Warsaw.

On the Friday evening service at the House of Prayer I suddenly, in the midst of the prayers, started to sob in a crescendo which went from quiet sobs to an hysterical loud crying. Father begged me to stop and not to disturb the Rabbi's praying by crying – but I just couldn't control myself and I continued to cry, with one picture before my tearful eyes: "I want grandmother Deborah!" I repeated these words hundreds of times. Father tried everything he could think of to quieten me down and stop me crying. He promised me that on Sunday we would go to Warsaw by train, and he will buy me a golden watch with a golden chain, which I hankered after. But I couldn't listen to his calming voice, and I repeated incessantly with bitter sobbing: "I want to go back to my grandmother Deborah." She was my mother's mother, a very prim and pious, thin, tall woman, who wore ancient yellow pearls – the colour of her skin. She was a kindly but severely religious woman, who would only give me a piece of cake and a little glass of cheery liquor (visniak) if I said my prayers and a chapter of the psalms before, while she stood by my bed.

I had not a great love for her as I had for my other grandmother, Chana. They both stayed with us and got on well together.

I didn't stop crying and sobbing for twenty-four hours. Even after my father borrowed a gold watch from a young man who stayed in the same Inn in the town where we were staying. He put it under my pillow, and he promised that he would buy me a nicer gold watch tomorrow in Warsaw! When we arrived from the station by carriage, the same Sunday, our shop was shut. An aunt came out and took me in her arms. My grandmother Deborah had died that same Friday evening when I began my terrible crying and longing for her.

CHAPTER SEVEN

Later my great-grandmother, Lipke, came to join us, and she was the one who spoiled me most.

She foretold that I should be a great and Holy Tzadik, and I shall live to see the days of redemption, and go forward to meet the Messiah, who must come any day now, for these are the days of Gog and Magog, when the great war will be raging – a sure sign of the coming of the Messiah. She was a little woman in a black, silken cap, interwoven with shiny beads. Her toothless face, shrivelled like an old apple, was constantly smiling. She could sew without glasses, and her hearing was very good. Once I overheard such a conversation between the two: She whispered something to Mother that I shouldn't hear, and my grandmother put her hand to her ear and said: "What do you say?" Several times my grandmother repeated the question and then said to her daughter: "Oi! Chana, you are no longer a Mentsch!"

When great-grandmother Lipke was taken ill, my aunt Lea took me by the hand, pushed away all the other great grandchildren, and brought me to her bed: "Bless him, this is your Rachmiltshe Eli's son!"

My grandmother took my hand with her bony fingers and said: I am not dying yet, let him bless me! She died a few days later. She was a hundred and five years old.

Just before she died I heard rumours and whisperings, which stopped when I was in the room. It was a dark mystery which I couldn't fully comprehend.

But once I heard the full story from grandmother, with tears streaming down on her wrinkled face, she divulged to me the terrible secret. A brother of hers who lived in Warsaw, who went off the right path, became a convert to Christianity, studied for the priesthood, and went to America. He became very rich, and finally became a Bishop in "*Frantz Francisco*" (as Grandmother called San Francisco). There had been going on a secret litigation she said, about his inheritance, which was supposed to be quite considerable, and he had no children. Lawyers were writing back and forth from New York and San Francisco to Warsaw, his father would have nothing to do with the inheritance of a Meshumed – the converted uncle.

On me, this dark secret made a tremendous impression. I was both horrified and delighted with the rebellion of my great uncle through his apostasy. And, when I later quarrelled with my aunt Chana, and wanted to annoy her for constantly pestering me about my neglecting the religious commandments, of which there are six hundred and thirteen Mitzvos, I couldn't think of anything more to say to her than: "I am going to be converted and marry a shikse (a Gentile girl). There was no more sinister threat for her, and this shut her up and she left me in peace.

Although I perfectly realised by then, after the murder of my father, that this apostasy was the worst, terrible crime I could commit, I was somehow secretly convinced that such an apostasy will show God what I think of Him for letting an innocent man like my father be killed in front of his son – on a Friday evening – the Sabbath.

Although my true faith was undermined, I still wanted to be a Chassidic Rabbi, and have followers travelling to me to be blessed, and to be dressed in a long silk gabardine, and a white "pekesha" on holidays. I wanted to be given presents and to dispense blessing and good wishes, with putting on hands, like my Rabbi, and say words of teaching and explaining the mysteries of the Kabbalah, although I had a very vague idea what it was and, what's more, I was not allowed to read the Zohar, the Mysteries of the Kaballah before I was twenty-five years old. Neither was I allowed to read such a book as the Guide for the Perplexed, by Miamonides, about which I learnt years later, from a contemporary Spanish philosopher, that there is only one title for a book on philosophy, and that Miamonides has already used that title. We used to call him by the odd sounding mellifluous name of his initials: – Rambam – Rabbeinu Moshe ben Maimon. It was also a forbidden book for the young and I had read that it was publicly burned by a Rabbi in Provence as a dangerous book. Although Miamonides was a most pious Rabbi, and an eminent physician in Spain, his book oddly enough written in Arabic and later translated by another hand into Hebrew, his book, unlike his encyclopaedic commentary and codification of the Bible and Talmud, was not allowed to be read by the young as it might lead one away from the straight path. Miamonides was on the "dangerous list", together with Mendelssohn's translation of the Bible, which was considered even more so.

Miamonides was philosophy, and we knew to what perilous paths philosophy can lead us. Didn't we read again and in the Talmud: "Know what to answer an Apikores" (an Epicurean). The Rabbi explained that there was actually such a Greek Philosopher, who was more dangerous even than Socrates and Apalton, as he called Plato, the wise men of Ionia. I immediately opted for Epicurus, and I loved the man, and I very early fell in love with being an Apikores – a non-believer. There was one Jewish Apikores we met in the Talmud, the great and mysterious Rabbi Elisha ben Abaia, who, together with two other Rabbis went into Paradise and he alone cut the roots of faith.

I was immensely sorry for this great, lonely and rebellious soul, who was no less than the master of the famous saintly Rabbi Meir, baal Hanes (miracle man). Very soon I discovered from another Apikores, a sickly son of a Melamed, an old bachelor who told me first about the tragic Marano Jew, Uriel d'Acosto, who was excommunicated by the Rabbis of Amsterdam, and Baruch Spinoza who refused to be silenced by the Community by offering him an "annuity" if he will not publish his philosophical writings.

And Spinoza too, that most saintly of all philosophers, whom I adored and who became, so to speak, my master, although I didn't properly understand him. But I knew that he was the first and most dangerous critic of the Bible; he was the first to point out that Moses could not have written himself about his own death. And that, in the Ethics, where ever he mentions Deus, he adds Sive Naturare. Spinoza, about whom Heine said that the coming generations looked through the glasses which he polished, was, to me, a guiding light out of the darkness of the narrow ghetto life. I could not forgive the Amsterdam

Rabbis for putting him in Chairem – excommunicating him – and for putting his books on the index of forbidden reading.

Together with a great number of other prohibited writings I began to buy masses of books: Goethe, Schiller, Heine, Lessing, and the classics of Yiddish and Polish literature, a two folio volume edition of Spinoza in a Polish translation. I had them bound and put together with other dangerous books on my table in my bedroom. I read them at night by candle-light, understanding very little of them.

One day, when mother was ill and I had gone out, Dr. Narewski visited her. He was the famous town doctor who put fear into the heart of his patients and their relations, and thus forced them to get better quickly. He was an original character, and all sorts of tales were told about him; that he charges big fees, but if he sees that the patient is poor, he leaves money under their pillow to buy medicine. He was a magnificent looking man with a curled brown moustache like a Polish nobleman, reminding one of a Rembrandt portrait. He had a very clear, shiny skin, and short, powerful hands of a pianist. In winter he was dressed in two fur coats, a seal-skin coat and on top of it a huge black sheepskin. He travelled in his own coach, with two brown horses and a driver. He would always sit on the left side of his old fashioned carriage, and everyone in town, Gentile or Jew, would take off his hat to him and he would wave back, leisurely, with one hand as if he were a priest blessing his people.

On this afternoon, when I was out and he came to visit my mother, he noticed the books on my table, standing in a row, and on top of each other. And the first books he picked up were, I was told, the two volumes of Spinoza. "Who reads that?" he asked in astonishment. Mother answered that the books were her son's.

"How old is he?"

Mother told him – fourteen years, and that he reads all day and until late into the night.

"Why, he will go mad. On zwarjuje, jak Boga Kocham (He'll go mad as I love God!)."

Mother and her neighbours and sister were frightened at these ominous words of the doctor, who was known to be a zealous Catholic.

"I'm going to take these books with me, and you must send up your son to me, and I'll see if he may have them back. These are very dangerous books for a young head, and can destroy his mind, if he isn't careful!"

Mother promised that she will send her boy up to the Pan Doctor. Doctor Narewski burst out of the house with the two volumes of Spinoza under his arms: "I am confiscating them, until I see him," he said.

When I came home later from my private lessons, mother greeted me in a flood of tears, and a wringing of hands at the terrible warning the doctor have given her.

"Why?" she cried, "Do you read such books, that even a Polish doctor considers too dangerous! He put the fear of God in me. How many times have I begged you not to read such dangerous books? Why do you, my only son, drive me prematurely to my grave? I have only got you left in my world, and you bring such shame on me, and make even a goyishe doctor angry?" But she was afraid even to mention that the doctor had shouted: "He'll go mad, on swarjuje." This I heard from my aunt Lea, who added that she knew a man, an old bachelor, whom I also knew, who went out of his mind and wandered the streets, grimacing and talking to himself. He was supposed to have gone mad reading the Cabalistic books.

"And you," said my aunt, in despair, "are going the same way, God forbid! Thank God he confiscated these dangerous books, and you mustn't forget to go up to him tomorrow. He wants to see you!"

The following morning, about ten o'clock, I went to his house, and waited patiently in the corridor for one of his patients to come out of his surgery. After a while he came out and said in a strong voice: "Nastepny (next)." I went in and told him who I was.

Dr. Nawrewski sat behind his large mahogany desk in front of the door, by the window. There was an old-fashioned dark red sofa behind him, over which hung an old oil painting, a portrait of a Polish nobleman, with a classical Polish moustache, wearing a sword and military tunic of the last century, with a lamb fur draped around his left shoulder. On his broad head, was a four cornered dragoon tall hat of the last century – a father or ancestor of the doctor; he almost looked like him.

Dr. Narewski did not shake hands with me, but motioned me to a chair in front of the desk. I sat down on the edge and waited.

"So you are the young man who reads Spinoza? How old are you?" I told him. "I," said the doctor with his bluff voice, "didn't read such Godless books when I was your age. Tell me. What do you understand about philosophy and Spinoza? Isn't he the fellow that wrote that there is no God? And that the Holy scriptures were written by men?"

My heart was, by now, almost in my mouth and it made me stutter. I was afraid that he would ask me what I understood in Spinoza. I really couldn't understand his philosophy myself, except that he was the father of Pantheism, the exact meaning of the word I didn't know, but for the easy formula that Spinoza made, the Universal God. But I somehow managed to remember a few sentences, i.e.: that virtue is it's own reward, and that one should love God but not expect God to love us in return. I also, luckily remembered a line of Novalis, who said that Spinoza was, "Gottbetrunken" (drunk with God). I admitted that it is difficult for me to understand the first and second parts of the *Ethics*, that is, perhaps, because I am ignorant of geometry, but I understand most of the chapters on emotion and of human bondage.

"But above all", I stammered, "I loved the man. And he was truly blessed," I added, explaining with some pride the Hebrew name "Baruch" for the Latin Benedictus, which means the same. I went on with my Talmudic sophistry, that I know that he is forbidden reading amongst religious Jews, but, I added, he was the liberator of many generations of Jews of my own background.

Dr. Narewski listened to me, with his broad, forceful face, with the grey-brown upturned moustache and strong heavy eyebrows over his small blue eyes. He smiled, and said: "But you are too young to burden your mind with such difficult books, which my own professor once said that even he could not understand or fully comprehend. Why don't you read the great poets, Mickiewidz, Krasinski, and the Polish classical novelists?"

I said that I had been trying to read them, but I prefer philosophy and history. And I am preparing myself to be a writer and philosopher, as soon as I get out from under my uncle's guardianship, who is a fanatical bigot! Only that last week, I told him, I had quarrelled with my uncle over a minor thing and I escaped, snatching a sharp knife from the table, and running through the fields into the woods and threatening that I will kill myself if he wont leave me in peace.

This was a bare-faced lie, because, when I ran away with the knife, which was true, I never really intended to kill myself. I just wanted to frighten my uncle. And it did seriously frighten him, because when he caught up with me, he spoke to me gently and out of breath, saying I should hand over the knife, and not drive him to his early grave, for my father – who was a saint – came to him in a dream and told him to look after me well; that I should be pious, and not wander from the straight path, and grow up a goy.

Dr. Narewski stretched out his hairy and well scrubbed hand and took pen and paper, made a gesture with his hand to me to be silent, and dipped the thick glass pen in a silver ink-stand.

"I'll write him a note. Ask him to come and see me. I'll give him a good talking to!" He gave me the letter in a closed envelope.

I got up and looked at the tall bookcase under glass, full of books. I asked him permission to look at them, and he added that I could borrow from these books whatever I liked, but remember to bring them back. I took several volumes, and I picked out two books, one by a Russian thinker, whose name I forget, and a book by a man whose name I had never heard, but which sounded to me significant, a book by Hypolite Taine – *A History of Italian Art,* if I remember rightly.

"You can borrow them, read them carefully, and ask me if you don't understand something."

I gave a last good-bye glance at the doctor, whose face and stature overawed me, and saw the profile of a small marble bust of the traditional head of Kosceszko, whose large statue was only recently put up in terracotta stone in the Market Place, where a Russian, enormous church had stood before, and was demolished as a hated symbol of Russia. He lent me the two books, and returned to me my two volumes.

"Whenever I am free come up and talk to me," were his last words to me. I couldn't wait to get down the street, where I opened and read the letter. In it he wrote that I am a very promising boy, destined to be somebody in the world, and that I must be given a chance to learn worldly science, and not only Jewish studies. And then came a phrase which flattered me highly. The doctor wrote that I am bound to be a second Meier Ezopowicz, the name of the Jewish romantic hero, by the popular woman writer, Eliza Orzeszkowa, who fights and longs to get out from a Jewish ghetto home. I liked the name of the "second Meier Ezopowicz", although I had not read the book but only heard about it.

I gave the letter to my uncle, and he pretended to be honoured that the great Polish doctor wrote to him, although I was sure that he didn't know who Meier Ezopowicz was.

A few days later I noticed the doctor passing in his carriage through our street, and he called my uncle from the pavement. I saw my uncle standing before the carriage in the middle of the road, with his cap in his hand and listening respectfully to the doctor. People from the shops looked at my uncle in his Jewish gabardine, standing, bareheaded, before the doctor. They wondered, probably, who might be so ill in the family that the doctor stopped his carriage – for it was not a common sight to see the Polish doctor speak in the street with a Jew in a long gabardine and Jewish, black cap.

The letter, and this stopping my uncle in the street, worked wonders. My uncle changed completely and began to treat me better, and stopped his fanatical persecutions.

Some weeks after I saw the doctor in his carriage passing the Warszowska Street where I lived. I took off my cap, and he gestured to me with his hand. He stopped the carriage and I went across to him. He asked me how things are with me and I told him, much better. He asked me where I was going, and I told him, home. He said: "Would you like to accompany me, and take a ride to see some of my patients?"

I got into his carriage on his right side, and he covered my feet with a leather frost-guard, over which was a white sheepskin. I felt immensely important, riding with the doctor in the same carriage, and hoped that many people will see me.

Chapter Eight

It was a clear, mild purple dusk, and the snow was already melting and getting dirty. But, as we turned the corner on the way to the railway station, the fields were covered with thick blue–white snow, and the pine forest was still laden with snow.

He asked me what I would like to study when I grow up. I said that I wanted to be a doctor: "Then you will have to work very hard!" he said. Ideally I wanted to be a poet and writer by that time, after having passed the stages of wanting first to be the Messiah, then, for a short period, a benevolent General – a kind of good-natured Napoleon, who would be kind to his soldiers. But when I was about ten years old I had a great desire to be a doctor. I even pretended that I was one. I got hold of some popular "Family Doctor" book and equipped myself with various ointments for rashes, boils, cuts and bruises; liniments and a bottle of iodine, bandages and cotton-wool; drops for appetite, which tasted like wine of rhubarbarum, castor oil for constipation, and a larger bottle for diarrhoea; drops for ear-aches and toothaches. I had modelled myself on a *feltcher*, Lubnan, who had a hairdressers shop next to our house, and also a surgery, which consisted mostly of a back room with a glass cupboard, equipped with surgical and dentist's instruments.

A "Feltscher" was a peculiarly Polish-Russian profession, he was licenced to pull teeth and attend the sick. They were originally male nurses and doctor's assistants for minor wounds and operations. Lubnan, a German Pole, was very popular, and naturally charged less than half the fees that doctors charged. He had several assistants who did the hair cutting and shaving in the large "salon". I used to assist him in the art of surgery, and especially tooth pulling from robust, big breasted Polish peasants, by holding their heads while he pulled the teeth.

Some young peasant women, dressed in their many coloured country dresses, with handkerchiefs round their heads, would scream like pigs, others could stand the pain without a murmur. When I was in the surgery with Herr Lubnan and assisted him in bandaging wounds, opening boils, or putting leeches behind the ears to draw blood, or even put hot compresses, with some black, smelly ointment, I thought that I was well on the way to becoming a doctor.

Secretly, however, I wanted to be a doctor, not so much to cure the sick and relieve suffering humanity, but because I knew that a doctor can look at naked women. I had a longing for undressed girls and women. Secretly I desired to touch them. And I remember when I was not even seven years old, I was longing to sleep in the same bed with our Polish maid, Stefa, and press myself to her warm smelling body – smelling of warm goat's milk and cheap powder and soap.

I don't remember from whom, but I got hold of a book on anatomy with illustrations and maps that opened up to show the whole human body. I thought this the mystery of mysteries. This lasted not very long, because as a colleague of mine, a first year student of medicine at the Warsaw University, took me with him to the operating theatre where an old woman was having an operation, I fainted – and had to leave the theatre.

But now, sitting beside Dr. Narewski in his old-fashioned carriage, drawn by two horses through the muddy streets of the town and over the snowy Kolejowa Street, which led to the railway station, I felt almost like a real doctor. He took me with him to a peasant's hut, with a straw covered roof. An old woman was breathing her last, and her husband and two daughters were crying silently. We went back through a different way, and came out by a clearing in the woods near a dirt road. It was snowing slowly in thick flakes, and the driver's hat and coat were getting white. In the carriage, the doctor covered me with a black lambskin and a heavy brown rug. Dr. Narewski was silent for a moment and suddenly said; as if to himself: "Poor woman, she hasn't got long to go!" Then he pushed down his black sealskin hat and began to recite quietly to himself, in a language I didn't understand or know. "You know what this is?" He said. "No," I answered, not even trying to guess. "Lord Byron's *Child Harold*. The great English poet!"

I had heard of neither.

I made a silent vow to learn English as soon as I can manage it. I was getting together something of a library, which I kept in the cupboard behind my father's Rabbinical and Talmudic books, of which I had been left a great number, but which I could neither understand – nor wished to know.

I read a huge amount of forbidden books, which one was not even allowed to keep in the same room as the religious books, bound in black with gold letters on its back. Father was a great buyer and reader of books. He hardly ever sat down to a meal without a religious book lying by his side.

★★★★★★★★★★★★★★★★★★★★★★★★

How Could Shakespeare Have Known Me?

★★★★★★★★★★★★★★★★★★★★★★★★

I wouldn't like to give the impression that I was a good, studious little boy, immersed in good books and in noble thoughts of my future poetical and literary exploits.

I was that, but constantly under the unforgettable scene of that tragic Friday evening. Though I felt that most deeply, I nevertheless could not bury in my heart the awful secret and horribly sinful thought, that I was not a little pleased that I was freed from my father's authority. Though, as I have told, he never laid a finger on me, and only very rarely shouted at me, for being disobedient, I nevertheless felt his authority oppressive and, at the same time, loved him more than my mother who lavished on me all her love, and spoiled me beyond words. I was not only her only Kadish, but her only child, and a ben Zikinim (son of old age). Her second marriage was to me a betrayal of my father, who had been murdered only a year before.

I couldn't distinguish between her marriage and a wicked woman found in adultery, which I knew from the Bible and Talmud deserves the severest punishment. An uncle, on my father's side, who told me secretly, that my inheritance is at stake, and whispered in my ear that my mother could still have a child by her second marriage, upset me so terribly, and put me to shame, that I was compelled to do a shameful deed. Under the pretence that I was caressing her, I kissed her cheek and at the same time touched her belly with both my hands to discover whether she is already pregnant. As her belly seemed to me to somewhat swollen, and the idea that she might be carrying a baby by that strange, hateful man, my stepfather, was repulsive to me. I came to the conclusion very quickly that she was not pregnant, and buried the secret discovery within me, as the most shameful suspicion I had ever had.

Mother gave me some money to buy oranges, a very rare and exotic fruit, which was also very expensive and hadn't been seen since the beginning of the War.

There was a witticism going round that if somebody is seen buying oranges, you naturally ask: "Who is ill at home?" Just as there was another folksy saying that if a poor man eats chicken, either he – or the chicken is sick!

I went in the afternoon to buy those luxurious oranges which I loved, particularly the sweet ones, which were called "blood oranges". On the way to the market I passed a small Jewish book shop that still sold all sorts of religious books, small prayer books bound in cedar wood with the imprint of Jerusalem on it, as well as cheap novelettes of robbers and princesses, of the terrible slaughter of whole communities by the murderous hoards of hitman Chumilnicki, which wiped out tens of thousands of Jews in small towns in the Ukraine in the years 1668-69, which were known as the Gezeires Tachve'tat, and made your blood curdle at the thought of what the Ukrainians, Kozaks and Russians were capable of doing. I bought none of these books, first because most of them I already knew, and the others I was simply afraid to read, they reminded me so much of my own father's murder before my own eyes, which I tried to – but couldn't forget. I spotted one small book in a grey paper cover, poorly printed, which was by a man called Karl Marx – of whom I had heard a lot, but never read, and the title of the book was "*The Communist Manifesto*". I bought it and paid for it with the money meant for the oranges, and I walked proudly from the book shop with Marx under my arm.

When I came home and mother asked me where the oranges where, I invented on the spot a lie, that they were all sold out.

But I didn't forget to write in my room, on the first page of the book: "Bought without the money for oranges" – with an eye for a future biographer, and to remind myself what a studious boy and omnivorous reader I was, sacrificing even delicious oranges for the higher pleasures of reading. I managed to amass quite a number of books, in three languages, many gained by the art of stealing. By this time I was an expert thief. Mother somehow didn't bother to find out where I got the money for all these books, bound and unbound. She knew that I got many from the public libraries; the Jewish ones from the public library of the Bund, and the others from the Polish library, which was kept by the paper shop. I even made an arrangement with the book-binder I know, to let me have on loan the new books before they were bound, as soon as they arrived from Warsaw. My immodesty, coupled with my zeal for reading, compelled me to be the first reader, at least in our town, so that I could show off my superior knowledge and say, nonchalantly: "Oh, yes! I know it!" Thus, I was the first reader, at least from my library, of the great Russians of Anatole France, of Knut Hamsun, of Strindberg and Nietzsche. Nietzsche, in particular, I loved, and I remember my first literary larceny, when I copied whole pages of "*Zarathustra*" and sent it as my own creation to a girl I thought I was in love with. What the poor girl must have thought of these mad writings, I never found out. I kept a little diary on my readings, and I remember that for long years I was ashamed of one remark I made about Don Quixote: I said that after reading the book – in a very poor Yiddish translation – that the book is silly, and I was so annoyed that I added: "If it were mine I would have burnt it!"

But in my own defence I must add that which I said about another book in the same diary. I had got hold of a second-hand copy of a shortened version of Shakespeare's works, in a shortened prose translation (probably a very bad one), with romantic illustrations on glossy paper. I somehow started with *Hamlet, Prince of Denmark*. I read it at one sitting and was astonished: How was it possible for a man with such an odd name as Shakespeare (written in Polish and Russian *SZEKSPIR*, and in Yiddish –), should have such a deep insight into my life and soul? My God, this man Shakespeare, that sounded to me both strange, comical and unmusical, should have known me so well. I saw in Hamlet the complete story of my life; my father, like Hamlet's, was murdered, though not by my uncle. My mother, it is true, was not as guilty as Hamlet's mother. Yet I saw myself a prince, who loved his father, the King (as, in a nutshell, were it not so in my bad dreams). I, too, suffered from terrible dreams like Hamlet, and I couldn't forgive my mother, whom I loved differently, for "betraying" my father, and marrying again, a second time, a man I couldn't look at. I, too, thought of – "To be – or not to be", though in a vaguer way, and found no consolation in philosophy. The only difference between me and Hamlet was that as a Jewish boy, I could not possibly have spoken to my mother in the rude manner of Hamlet. How can a man speak like that to one's own mother? And call her such unspeakable names as, Whore? I couldn't imagine a Jewish son speaking like that to this mother.

By that time I found out with deep disappointment that Shakespeare was definitely not a Jew, as I naturally assumed every great poet to be.

That you can see the touch of megalomania and plain narcissism in me to have identified myself with Hamlet, not knowing that generations of young men all over the Western world must have looked upon themselves as potential Hamlets. And I remember my sudden decision: If ever I shall become a writer and write something great, I shall use the name of Hamlet as my pseudonym. This I divulged in great secrecy to a school fellow, Moishe, to whom I had to explain who Hamlet was, and why he was so like me, except that he was not a Jew.

What made me more certain than ever that Shakespeare was not a Jew, was after reading the *Merchant of Venice*, after which I also read some commentaries by Jewish critics on this play and discussions as to whether Shakespeare was an anti-Semite or not. The critics were divided on this problem and, if I remember rightly, Heine thought that Shylock's famous monologue was a vindication of the Jew, and saved the play. I, on the contrary, thought that the play was not only anti-Semitic, but absolutely nonsensical. For Shakespeare, not having known a real Jew, tried to compete with the then popular anti-Semitic un-Jewish *JEW OF MALTA*, a really stupid and blood-curdling play. What prevented Shakespeare's play from being absolutely stupid, was his genius, and, unlike Marlow of Shylock; his sheer genius was driving him on and the words came tumbling down – like the walls of Jericho – on the age-old hatred of this persecutors, although the name Shylock became a loathsome word through generations and had done immense harm to the Jewish people.

To me the lie of the play lay in the fact that, not only was so blood-thirsty a Jew an impossibility, but even that there was in Venice such a Jew who demanded a pound of living Christian flesh; the Jews of Venice would have excommunicated him or stoned him to death for Chilul Hashem, by desecrating the name of God, and putting to shame the whole Jewish people. However, I had other worries than Shakespeare, nevertheless Hamlet overwhelmed me, and I was going round in a trance, imagining myself as the suffering Prince of Denmark.

I had then two teachers for Latin and Mathematics, of which I prided myself to be ignorant, and couldn't understand how, from Plato to Kant and Spinoza, philosophers thought mathematics of such prime importance.

My teacher of Polish was the son of my Hebrew teacher, a Lithuanian named Zuk, whom I rather liked. He recommended me to read some children's books first, to get acquainted with the Polish language, and he brought me one afternoon a little book called Hansel and Gretel. After the Talmud and the beautiful legends of the Messiah and the great Chassidic Rabbis – you can imagine what I felt, reading such a barbarous and stupid story as Hansel and Gretel, whose meaning I utterly failed to understand. It was frightening and senseless and cruel, and I didn't see how such a story can improve the mind of a fifteen year old boy, who knew whole passages of the Bible and Talmud, with difficult commentaries, almost by heart.

I couldn't help being puffed up with pride when I made nearly an hour's long speech, and delivered a complicated Talmudic exposition, with sophisticated commentaries of such great authorities as Rashi and the Tosephot, at my Bar Mitzva, and was complimented by everyone for my Talmudic casuistry and eloquence. Mother listened with the other women of my family in a separate room, divided from the men by a white curtain, to keep men and women separated, according to custom. And I had myself overheard a number of people saying to my mother, after my speech, standing on top of a chair, "Your son, blessed be the Name of Him in Heaven; your son is growing like his father, peace be upon him, and to longer years. He's already an *illui* (a genius)." This didn't help my modesty.

But even better than at learning obscure pages of the Babylonian Talmud, I was an adept at thieving! I could not only get out money from mother's purse, but I learned how to open with a pen-knife, the cash box in our shop, where I could get away with quite big sums, tens and twenties of marks or zloties. Once, I remember, I ran out with my loot into the out-house and discovered with a shock that amongst the money was a 100 Zloty note! I suddenly started to tremble with fear, and decided to put it back. It was more difficult than stealing it, because I went about it in a most hypocritical way. I dropped it behind the counter and, with complete disregard for truth, said: "You must have dropped it," and gave Mother back the 100 zlotys. Mother was so delighted by my honesty that she gave me a reward of five zlotys!

I must admit that after such a demonstration of honesty I couldn't help asking myself inwardly; Why am I so clever? A question I asked myself a number of times, and being immensely pleased when I saw, even years later, on this same question: "Why am I so clever?" in Nietzsche's short book, "*Ecce Home*", which fell into my hands.

However, not to give the impression that I was a thoroughly wicked liar and, I must say, that my highly developed art of stealing was not completely immoral: I was generous too with my mother's money. Whenever a poor woman came into the shop and I was by the cash desk, I would give her change from five zlotys, as if she had given me 20 zlotys for the groceries, pretending that I didn't remember how much she had given me. They never corrected me – or refused the change!

On Tuesdays, when the town's poor went round to the Jewish houses to beg for their weekly charity, I would clandestinely give them double – or more than my mother would give them. There was one toothless, thin woman who would lift her hands and eyes to Heaven, and shout blessings at me, and say that she had never seen such good-heartedness and generosity in her whole life, and that God will surely bless me until I am a hundred and twenty years.

Is there any wonder that I had a too high opinion of myself? It took me some time to realise that I was in reality very selfish, obstinate, and sometimes even insolent to others. Very soon I discovered that my goodness and generosity of giving to the poor was nothing but a conceited selfishness, and it was an additional flattery to my pride: You can see how suffering humanity really affected me.

I often envied myself my good luck, my so called riches, which I inherited, and the innate sharpness of mind and my dexterity in stealing, which I developed to a fine art. I was even pleased with my looks – at least I thought I am not ugly or crippled. My face, although sharp and thin, was pale, and my eyes, though small, were black and deeply set, and because my face was broad on top and narrow at the chin, they called it "*Kezel*" – "little cheese", as it was the shape of a Polish heart-shaped white farm cheese. But I thought that I am not attractive to girls, for when they did look at me they giggled ..

Chapter Nine

It was at that time when I began to have fantasies about girls; I vaguely guessed something about sex, but I thought babies came out of the navel, and that boys came out from fathers and girls from mothers. About that time I bought a second-hand book, with coloured, detailed numbered diagrams of male and female organs. This book opened my eyes and, although I had seen my father and other men in the public baths, I had never seen my mother, and she, like other women, remained a dark mystery, and every one of them hated to be touched, including my stepsister. But one day in a neighbouring court-yard I saw a girl playing with children, and sitting on top of the steps, her legs apart, her skirt up, and I saw her pudenda. My eyes were glued to her pubic hairs, and I was horribly fascinated and disgusted by the *tabu* and shattering sight.

Two things interested me most – girls and books. I read voraciously whatever fell into my hands. I must have been reading some eight to ten hours a day, neglecting my home-work and the exercises of my lessons from the two private tutors who were coming to teach me Russian, German and Polish, and a Hebrew teacher who "rehearsed" me in my Bible, Talmudic and rabbinical classic studies. I got a teacher for mathematics, a subject I really hated; I just couldn't understand why 2 and 2 should make four, because I saw somewhere that a philosopher said that two lambs and two lions *don't* make four! On the other hand I have read a wit who said that 2 and 2 is, with Rothschild, not four – but 22!

I did my own research in biographies, and noted carefully who amongst great writers and poets disliked mathematics or were plain bad at it. To my great disappointment I found that two of my most loved philosophers, Plato and Spinoza were both great mathematicians, and with Plato mathematics was the most divine science Man was given. And although my complete lack of geometry made it abstruse for me to understand his first chapters of his "Ethics", I could swim in the cool seas of the later parts "On The Passions" and "Of Human Bondage".

In addition, I took Spinoza, who was absolutely tabu, as my guide and master in my growing revolt against the tyranny of the Bible, which weighed heavily upon our minds and souls. We wanted to free ourselves from the bondage of the relentless Torah and – the – dry Talmud. But I must say that I loved the melody and the sing-song of the Talmud, more, than its sophisticated problems (the Talmud is never read, but chanted with a special oriental chant, which might have come down from Babylon and the Moors from Andalusia, through the forest of Bukovina, Poland, and Ukraine and Lithuania).

Even the Bible is not read but chanted with special chants, and the prayers on the Sabbath and on the Holy days have their special traditional chant. The Bible, which is "learned" every week, chapter by chapter, for the whole year until the end, and on Sabbath Bereishis, you start again with Genesis, so that when I was about ten years old I had already read the whole five books of Moses, five or six times, not to mention several books of the prophets and the "writings".

The special teacher of the Talmud at that time was a well known Talmudist in town, who came to our house, because he was a failed business man of a very good family, Rabbi Chaim Vishnitzen by name, who was my father's distant relative, and whom father wanted to support without putting him to shame as taking "charity". He had a dark reddish long beard, and his breath, when he was sitting close to me, had a most pleasant smell of sweet almonds. Later I was told that people with such breath show signs of a secret illness. But the most remarkable thing about him was his high forehead with permanent three broad wavy deep lines across. I envied him his "thinkers" forehead like a philosopher, and often I tried to imitate him and make my forehead lined, by holding it, sometimes for hours, with two fingers of both my hands. But it didn't work – the moment

I took away my fingers my forehead became childishly smooth again. Moreover, my forehead was very short!

Envying the man who had a philosopher's high, wrinkled forehead, I remember asking the next-door barber to shave off the corners of my hair at the temples and make the hair-line higher. And, of course, this didn't last long, for within a few days my hair grew back again. I envied people who wore glasses; I thought, with a high wrinkled forehead and a pair of glasses, I too will look like a philosopher or a poet, and I was careful not to go out of my house without a sizable book under my arms. I was terribly vain.

I didn't go round moaning in despair of my terrible sins, as did St. Augustine in his confessions, who thought God will never forgive him for the terrible crime of stealing pears from somebody's garden, and even more of his greater sin, of making a girl pregnant, and living with her and her bastard son for many years. My conscience was not as heavy as his. But as there was a break in my communications with God, and I lost my terror of Heaven, I was all to conscious of my minor sins; as handling money on the Sabbath, not waiting six hours to eat butter or cheese after having eaten meat; walking longer distances on the Sabbath than it is permissible – less than half a mile; not to mention the sins of riding on the Sabbath – an even greater sin; or cutting a branch from a tree, and a hundred such transgressions of do's and don'ts, of which there are 613 mitzvoths, all enumerated in a religious book composed in the middle ages and known as the "*Schulchan Aruch*" (the prepared table), a book that became as obligatory as the Bible and the Talmud; a book I particularly disliked, for there was nothing in the world a Jew can do on the Sabbath except to pray, to listen to the Torah, and eat fish and meat, prepared on the Friday.

Although I had lost all fear of Heaven, I nevertheless still practised my old art of trying to get used to Hell by putting my hand or fingers in a burning candle – or on the red-hot coals of the kitchen fire. It hurt a bit but it was better to be on the safe side and not be plunged into the burning fires of Hell (which, I was told, does not work on the Sabbath and gives the sinners a twenty-four hour respite). Once I began to read forbidden dangerous books – there was no stopping me. I finished all the books in the Jewish Socialist library of the Bund, which had most of the Yiddish writers, Peretz, Mendele, Sholem Aleichem, and Asch. I read history, biography, and translations from the French, Scandinavian, German and of course Russian and Polish writers.

When my teacher started teaching me Polish and German, he gave me first children's books. As I have already mentioned, the story of Hansel and Gretel I thought, not only stupid but terrible; to cut off the finger of the boy to see if it was yet fat enough to eat! How could this blood curdling story be of any instructive or moral use to a child?

One day I found a book of Emanuel Kant who, I was told, was one of the few men who changed philosophy. It was his *Prelegomena*. I bought it and asked my teacher to dictate to me from it.

"But you wont understand a word," he said. "I don't understand Hansel and Gretel either," I answered, "and I'd rather understand Kant, and not understand such childish drivel, as the stories you dictate from!" My teacher was puzzled. It was about that time that I asked my teacher, Zuk, that he should write a sort of sketch to a portrait of me, as a sort of character study. In a kind of secret anticipation as to what people will be writing about me when I have grown up into a famous man! I was convinced that I am growing into a genius, and if I couldn't prove that I am a genius already, then I begged my teacher to write the truth. A few days later he handed me a few pages from a notebook.

"Examination of a Young Character" I think he called it. I read it avidly when I was alone. I was amazed at his understanding of me. He said, if I remember rightly, that I show potentialities of talent. He did not flatter me. But I was suffering from the disease of being a rich only son. Generous to a point but, as a Frenchman said about modesty, only in order to be additionally praised. But, he continued, I am also lazy, slothful and vain. Not a word of flattery, but no denial that I am a "dreamer" with my head in the clouds. That I must not rely solely on my quick understanding and excellent memory, but must work and work on my development and must not be so cocksure of myself as to imagine I understand a lesson just by reading it and memorizing it once only. He told me that I have a generous character, but I am inclined to be arrogant and look down on other boys. But I have a "Jewish Heart", and have compassion with those who suffer, though I am also too conscious of what a special boy I am. Though he put down a few hard-hitting truths, he was mildly severe and didn't flatter me at all. I think my teacher used the words, egocentric and narcissistic, which I didn't understand and he had to explain to me.

I was not insulted nor annoyed by this criticism, on the contrary, I thought it fair, and that I was almost aware of my failings, with the additional pride that I saw through my own character and couldn't deceive even myself.

In my fantasies I was still at the age of wanting to be a doctor. But what kind of doctor? Having seen Motel Waiszawwiak, a huge, common Jew, who lived in our house on the top floor, who served as the driver in charge of heavy sacks and barrels that arrived by goods train; one Friday evening he had a complete collapse, started screaming like a savage and wanted to throw himself into the deep well which stood in the corner of our courtyard. His wife struggled with him and prevented him, with the help of neighbours, from throwing himself down the black open well, which was no longer used. I was a witness to this macabre scene, and the man's wild eyes, distorted face and terrifying screams made a shattering impression on me, and for days I couldn't think of anything but those screams.

I had experiences of other men and women, town lunatics, some quite harmless, who were roaming the street and did no harm, except for frightening the children. Also once, when I went out during the day, to the House of Prayer, I saw the idiot son of a neighbouring Jew all alone (he didn't see me), behaving in a strange way; he stood by a long table and repeated obscenities about the copulation of his father and mother. I had heard these obscenities before, but this was the first time that I heard them repeated in a maniacal frenzy by a sick mind. It was a shaking experience, and I was terribly frightened, especially when I knew that there was nobody in the House of Prayer, and I stood outside secretly listening to him. I was completely shaken, and then and there, I decided that if I became a doctor, I shall study psychiatry. If I will discover how and why man loses his mind and behaves like a beast, I shall begin to understand the mysterious workings of man's mind.

It was at this time that I was taken to a woman by an older boy, the son of a neighbour, who initiated me into the mystery of sex, which began slowly to rise in me, but which I couldn't understand. At almost the same time there was born in me another emotion, which seemed to me to be something quite different, and even more powerful than sex itself: Love. I had been reading about young people, mostly poets, in love with girls. I had read a number of novels about love, which I thought rather romantic and silly. I was no longer a romantic, I was of the post-war generation, and I remember that I couldn't even read Tolstoy, and I put him aside. What was the use of reading Tolstoy – or Balzac, when they couldn't prevent the War? I remember throwing away Balzac – what has he got to teach me after 1914-18?

Towards the end of the War, I watched once for a whole day, columns of German field hospital lorries, moving through the main street of our town, straight from the front, with hundreds of wounded soldiers, many without legs or hands, or with bandaged heads so that not even their eyes were visible. The backs of the lorries were open and I could see them, some with bloody rags around their legs and hands, and some faces monstrously distorted and bloody. I watched from the steps of our house for hours, until my legs gave way and I vomited.

This was the first time that I saw the bloody results of War. To be a revolutionary and anti-war was, to me, the highest ideal a man can have.

Who can think of such an old-fashioned luxury as love? Towards the end of the War in the East, we began to read about the rise of the revolutionary sun in Russia, after a long dark night. We read about Lenin and Trotski on one side; the Red Army which has abolished the hated Regime of the Tsar. We were full of hope and fear. It was impossible not to be carried away with enthusiasm for the Russian Revolution. On the other side, we read in the papers about the pogroms on Jewish populations in hundreds of towns and villages, particularly in the Ukraine, which were attacked by the white general's armies of Petlura and Denikin.

Barely two years afterwards the Polish Army, under Pilsudski attacked Russia, and when the Red Army was stopped at the Vistula by Warsaw, we were expecting the Red Army any moment in our little town. Some towns welcomed the Bolsheviks with open arms. Whatever the Red Army did, with all the expropriations and confiscations, we were sure of one thing – there would be no pogroms, and the Bolsheviks will protect us from Polish troops and marauders.

To tell the truth we were apprehensive at the outbreak of Polish independence, the Government and practically the whole Polish press was violently anti-Semitic and I remember that sometimes, in autumn, after the Germans had left, riding back from some village where a cousin rented a big orchard from a Polish landowner, there were with us several Jewish travellers, who were factors and middlemen for Polish noblemen; they talked among themselves and I heard one saying: "The Poles will destroy us all. There will be pogroms in the towns. Nobody will escape from their hands!" The peasants in the fields stopped in the middle of their harvesting and gazed at us, making threatening gestures with their hands across their throats – that they will slaughter us and all the Jews. Even the Jewish newspapers were not allowed to report these pogroms. The very word was censured, and instead they printed such euphemisms as "riots", "unrest", and for the worst "excesses". And so, when you got the papers from Warsaw, you saw sometimes whole white columns with news censured – or just a headline: "Disturbances" in Poznan, or Raddau, or Bialystok, Wilno. The first of these cities became known for the *Hallerczyki*, as the Army in former Russia, under General Haller, a notorious anti-Semite, was known. Jewish passengers were thrown from running trains, and old Jews had their beards torn out by soldiers, and left with bloody faces and ears.

This reminded us of a less brutal way of Europeanizing the Jews by cutting their long beards with scissors. And I well remember my father coming home from the ritual bath with half his coat cut off by German soldiers who caught Jews in the streets, and cut off their beards, and their coats, which Polish Jews usually wore down to the ankles.

One day my mother having gone to a relation's wedding in winter, came back from her journey with her face and hands as yellow as lemons. She was seriously ill, and the doctor visited her several times.

He prescribed all sorts of medicines for her, and there was talk of an operation. Our aunts and uncles despaired, as if they had something to hide from me. And one day an uncle said to me the dreadful word, which in Polish and Yiddish sounds even more sinister: "She has "rak" – cancer."

When I came home and looked at my mother, I was overcome with emotion, but did not cry, just as my mother never cried when I was in her room. Once when I was lying on a canvas chair in her room I heard her cry bitterly and quietly, while I fell asleep with a dream I remember to this day.

The dream was of a crowd of Jews, reminiscent of a picture by a painter Hirschenberg, driven by Cossacks in horses into expulsion, with a Rabbi in a Talis with a Torah in his arms leading the procession of old and young men and women from a small town. They stopped every few minutes, as a verse of melody, which turned into a lament, with the refrain: "Oh! For the sake of the Holy Sabbath!" Which was followed by a weird beating of a drum and a brass instrument, which I couldn't distinguish. The words were my mother's, who kept repeating the prayer: "Oh! For the sake of the Holy Sabbath, for the sake of the Holy Sabbath; for the sake of the Holy Sacred Days!" Not after so many years have I forgotten the melody which I had never heard before.

I went to see Dr. Narewski. Patients were waiting for him, but I went straight in. I didn't ask him whether mother can be cured, and he, without being asked said briefly: "I can't help her. Ask your Rabbi to pray for her!" He was a believing Polish Catholic, and prayer, even from a Chassidic Rabbi in whose miracles he had faith, was all he could offer me in consolation. I no longer believed in anything, having even tried a cure by a neighbouring Polish peasant woman to whom I was sent. She told me to put wax in mother's urine and see what comes out of it. And to put a flea in her food. I looked for a flea, found one, and squashed it into a cooked prune and gave it to mother, without telling her what she was eating. But she still didn't get better. That night after I had been to the doctor, I slept with my stepfather, and I shivered all night – just as I had shivered the night when my father was murdered.

74

But this pain of losing my mother seemed infinitely worse. In my heart I must have loved her more than my father. And the thought that now I shall be left all alone in the world was too much to bear.

I was overtaken by a terrible pity because of the pain that my mother suffered. But, having read a little philosophy, I tried to console myself with the thought that greater men and women than my mother died younger than she. I couldn't think of anybody who died prematurely, then of Spinoza and Theodor Herzl, whom I loved most, one who taught us not to laugh and not to cry, but to understand, and the other, who was a beautiful legend of a new modern prophet of his people.

Then, one afternoon when I stood at my mother's bed and looked at her yellowish face, it suddenly shrunk to the size of a man's fist. I was so overcome with horror that I broke down and went up to the window and cried bitterly, and sobbed for her and myself.

Here I stood sobbing, amidst all these old and young people, who gathered in the room to say psalms: a sure sign that the end is nigh. I forgot all my premature imaginings of being a great man, and I became a young "round" orphan in despair over his dying mother. From now on I am all alone in this vast, strange, frightening world.

Chapter Ten

A gain I followed her coffin, which was carried on a black wagon, dragged by two old horses draped in black covers with only holes for their eyes. There were so many people crying and wailing around me, that I couldn't see her, or how they put her in her grave near my father's, which was also hidden from me. I said Kadish, with a great attempt not to break down and forget the words; an uncle, who stood near me took the precaution of repeating it to remind me of the Aramaic prayer, word perfect. Perhaps here I should mention how conscious I was of the tragic-comic irony in my young life.

Relatives, friends and neighbours, were crowding the house, eating hard-boiled eggs dipped in ashes, as tradition prescribes, and the friends are allowed to "comfort" the mourners with words of praise for the dead, their piety and generosity, and how I, the only Kadish and "round orphan", wont have anybody to care for me. They bewailed me as if I had just died, and praised me for my delicacy, generosity and love and respect for my parents, and what will now happen to me, all alone in the world with nobody to love me, considering the love and care and prayers they lavished on me while waiting for me to be born.

I was both deeply embarrassed and flattered at the same time, and my self importance and pride swelled in my heart. But my eyes were dry.

I was sitting on a bed in the sitting-room and couldn't cry – and, suddenly, I felt a terrible urge to relieve myself! But how can one pass through so many sobbing and mourning people, mostly women, to so vulgar and banal a need as peeing amidst such tragedy? It was somehow so incongruous a thing, that I went into the dark shop which was closed. I was ashamed to pass to the outside lavatory – mourners just cant perform such banal functions! At the corner of the shop was a huge bottle of vinegar essence, which was deadly poison, having heard that people died by just drinking a little bit of this essence. There was an empty bottle next to it – and I relieved myself into this bottle. Just as I was in the midst of emptying my bladder, my uncle rushed in to see what I am doing alone in the dark shop, and being ashamed that I might be caught in such a tragic moment, and being afraid that my uncle will notice the urine in the bottle, I threw it down and broke it. My uncle, having discovered me with the broken bottle, was sure that I was going to poison myself with the essence of vinegar and that only he had saved my life by dragging me away. Shouting: "Lord of the World! What are you going to do? Don't you know that this is the greatest of sins?" He took me by the hand and triumphantly brought me back into the sitting-room, telling everybody how – "he saved the boy's life, who nearly poisoned himself!" I let him believe that I had broken a bottle of poison, not to spoil his heroic act in a mock tragedy, which was, to me, my first tragic-comedy of errors and irony.

After this scene I bravely bore the compassion and sorrow, the sympathy of the neighbours and family, when I passed in the street, conscious of the fact that I am something unique – a round orphan of a wealthy Jewish house, who lost his innocent father through evil men, and his mother who had died of grief and regret – for marrying again!

My uncle moved into our home to take care of me, and my Aunt Lea, who was quite confused about the world around her, a simple woman who could barely read her prayers and a Yiddish collection of Bible stories, but she was devoted to me with all her heart, because I was the only son of her most beloved brother who, in her eyes, died a martyr's death. He had brought her up since she was a young girl and had given her a dowry, as he had to all his younger relations. Uncle, who was not a bad man but whom I disliked because, being ignorant he couldn't distinguish what was forbidden by Jewish law, and what was not, according to custom. He didn't know a word of the Talmud or any other difficult book, yet he travelled to a Chassidic Rabbi of Skierniewice, where he happened to be born, the Rabbi of my father who had also taken me to visit him.

It was decided by a sort of family council that he and my aunt Lea should move into our house and take over the shop, look after me, until I found a nice Jewish girl who would make me a rich Jewish bride. I was fifteen years old. I continued my studies of the Talmud and worldly learning with my two teachers. I was left a big house where, besides us, there were several tenants who paid monthly rents, and which I spent on "luxuries" and books, and various mechanical toys and games of which I was very fond.

One poor woman cried that she hasn't got any money to pay the rent – so I told her not to worry.

It was about that time, after mother's death, that I began to feel mysterious passions and longings in my body, which as I soon discovered from reading popular books on puberty, was the beginning of my sexual awakening.

But I didn't know what to do about it. Until one summer afternoon, sitting on the sofa of a woman, who must have been some ten years older than I, with magnificent breasts, initiated me. She was, it seemed to me, an enormous woman with thick fair hair in a bun, and long shapely legs. She was engaged to be married to a much older man and she practised her jealousy on me.

She was the cousin of a painter whom I didn't know, but who lived in a nearby town. She showed me a self portrait of his in charcoal which seemed to me to be very good. She told me that he is going to Germany to study art, and that he will one day be a great painter. Her prophesy was not wrong as it turned out, for we became very great friends thirty years later in London. His name was Yankel Adler.

It was this handsome woman who initiated me in to the mysteries of sex. She it was who gave me the first kiss which sent an electric current through my spine, and weakened my legs. This kiss lasted God knows how many minutes, and I thought that my soul is being stifled with my breath. This was the first kiss that awakened my manhood, and I was so overcome with emotion, that I didn't know what to do with myself. I was still inwardly afraid that such a kiss must make a woman pregnant. That this is the real "thing".

I was particularly fond of my reaction – my *poetic* reaction – to this kiss, for her mother was frying potato latkes (pancakes), a favourite dish of mine, in the kitchen. She went into the kitchen and brought me one with sugar on top, and then left me alone. I tried to eat it and took a bite, but after such a kiss, the pancake tasted vile! I spat it out and threw it out of the window, which was open. I was glad, as I said, to have discovered in myself such a disgusted reaction to the prosaic, oily, taste, after such a lofty, romantic feeling –– Maybe I am a poet? Since then, whenever I feel a base taste after a lofty emotion, I am reminded of the taste of the potato in that oil pancake, and I remember that first passionate kiss that almost split my spine in two.

Another similar feeling of disgust and shame with myself was sometime later, when I became the editor of a one page local, provincial weekly newspaper, which was published in a neighbouring town called Piotrków. When I started writing, I started with journalism in which I satirised the local assimilationist manufacturers who despised the workers and simple people, whom they exploited, and their Yiddish which was the Jewish language of the people. Although I knew Hebrew – I was a passionate Yiddishist and, of course, a socialist, which I had been long before I read Marx, or other social writers.

It seemed to me such a true and obvious solution, the only ethical solution in a world of exploitation, meanness, hunger and suffering of the poor. I was, naturally, ashamed to belong to a richer class who, though my father didn't get rich from exploiting workers but through his own hard work, was nevertheless, one of the town's wealthy men, although a kind and charitable man.

Very early I began to ask him august questions about the prayers, and how we only pretend that we are charitable. So, I remember asking father once, whether it is not hypocritical to repeat several times a day a prayer after meals for a psalm that says: "I was young, and I am now old, and have never seen a righteous man forsaken, and his children begging for bread." And I asked my father why he tells an untruth every day, when across the road lives a good man, a tailor, whose children and wife are always hungry, not to mention the tailor, himself, about whom a local wit had said that – if not for the fact that he has to fast every Monday and Thursday, he would long ago have perished from hunger. I remember father looking at me as if he were at a loss to answer me, and he finally came out with a little contrived and unconvincing reply: "It seems that we shall not see in *The World to Come*, such righteous people forsaken and his children starving? Inwardly he was probably feeling proud of the "profundity" of my unorthodox question, and at the same time embarrassed by his lame answer.

However, I remember the answer did not satisfy me, as my faith in the Bible and God was beginning to falter. Though my fear of the Bible was gone I didn't yet understand it's poetry. I was beginning to get bored by its repetition, for by that time I must have read, or rather "learned", the whole Bible six or seven times, finishing it every year – from Genesis to the death of Moses.

I loved the Sabbath, though we had so many restrictions there was at least one thing in it's favour – there was no cheder, no house of prayer, and we could go, after the rich Sabbath meal, to play, provided we didn't break branches from trees or throw stones. But we loved the Holy days, particularly the Festival of Passover.

Passover usually began with a complete "revolution" in our household. Not only were all the walls inside re-painted or repaired by house painters on high double ladders, on which they would cross the room from wall to wall, as if on stilts, but the whole house would be cleansed and windows washed, and even the whole stove would be cleaned, or made Kosher, with red hot coals inside and outside for hours on end. Then there was the baking of Matzos, which I loved to watch, for about a week or two in advance. Usually the baker and his help were at the oven, which had also been Koshered by a special fire of logs, and the women would knead and roll out the dough on long clean tables, and young girls would puncture the flat matzos (so that they shouldn't rise), and carry them quickly to the ovens where they were shoved in three or four at a time. But a day or two before Passover, my father joined the other Chassidim, and baked himself the Matzos Shmirah, the specially "guarded" matzos, which were not entrusted to women, but it was a holy obligation, a mitzvah, to bake them oneself, and my father suddenly became a baker, and shoved the matzos into the oven. Among the Chassidim the baking of Matzos was not to be left to the women, or to professional bakers, but was a special privilege which they themselves performed. Even the water being fetched from the well by pious men, kneaded and rolled with a wooden hand roller, and rushed to the oven without losing a precious second, in case the matzos should rise and thus become doubtful unleavened bread. These Matzos Shmirah were only baked by the very pious Chassidim themselves.

Another ceremony, which children liked, was the looking in corners and hidden places for pieces of bread and crumbs, which would be entrusted, clandestinely, to put away in order that my father, who with a candle and goose feather wing, and a big wooden spoon, would gather them up and burn the "Chometz" in the court yard.

Passover (Pessach), I loved more than any other holiday. Not only did we have new clothes, overcoats, and new caps and shoes, and not only because of the Spring in the air, but the traditional foods we had to eat. Delicious Matzos balls with chicken soup, which father would not eat on the first two days of Festival, and the four cups of wine for each one of us, and one cup which father would fill ceremoniously for the Prophet Elijah and set it aside, on top of the table, and which nobody touched.

For, after beginning the Hagada in the traditional sing-song, father, in a white special robe, at the top of the table, in a half-lying position on a specially bedded out chair with cushions, symbolizing the freedom of an Oriental patriarch lying down to his meal, would intone from the Hagada the first lines, uncovering the four Matzos that were lying in a linen, embroidered bag with four divisions, and, in the ancient melody would repeat the ceremonial Aramaic: "Khu, Cachum Anin." ("This is the poor bread that our Fathers have eaten in the land of Egypt. Let all who are hungry, come and eat.") And in the last Passover we had even a guest, a German Jew serving in the German Army.

After the four questions which I had to ask father before the fourth cup of wine is drunk, there is told the story of the liberation from Egypt, and then a little traditional ceremony which was both awe inspiring and, to me, full of mysterious terror.

I had to go and open the door for the invisible prophet Elijah, who visits every Jewish house on the first night of Passover, and invisibly drinks from his cup of wine, that has been poured out for him. It was my privilege, as the youngest son, to open the front door out into the dark court-yard. Having heard so often the abominable blood lie, that Jews kill Christian children to mix their blood with the matzos, and that this horrible crime happened usually before the start of Passover, when murdered children are being laid at the door of unsuspecting innocent Jews, I was trembling with fear that I might find such a body outside our door. This story was still so real to me, ever since my childhood when I had lived through the days of the Bailis trial, and which ended unexpectedly with the freeing of Mendel Bailis from this monstrous blood accusation, in spite of the famous Russian accusers Prensitis and Shmakof who proved, with false quotations from the Talmud, that Jews must use the blood of Christians, preferably children, for their Matzos on Passover.

I used to run back quickly to my father at the head of the table, not even waiting to close the door, and somebody else had to do it for me. The thought of what might happen to me if I really did discover a dead body behind the door, frightened me so much, that, these few seconds of opening the door for Elijah, was to me a real nightmare. From early childhood we were told about these libels, and we read about it in histories and folk tales, we trembled when we heard or read about it, and with that nightmare we grew up. That it left it's deep mark on our souls, there is no doubt. Together with this nightmare there was closely connected the death of Jesus, the prime cause of all our sufferings and persecutions.

Instinctively, before even knowing anything about the history of Jesus, we were, deep in our hearts, convinced that the crucifixion of Jesus was as much a lie as the accusation of the blood-libel. That this most cruel way of punishing was *not* a Jewish but a Roman way of sentencing guilty rebels, was an historical fact. We were so sure of our innocence that we thought were it not for the Romans and the first Christmas, Yishu – or Jesus – would have been considered a primitive Chassidic Rabbi, and perhaps a prophet. As to his being the "Son of God" – we were not at all shocked. Everyone of us prayed to "*Our Father*" in Heaven – "*Uvinn She'bashomain.*" This was one of the first prayers that I could remember. We were *all* God's children.

The nightmare of Jesus and his crucifixion came to me most poignantly on Passover, in which the fear of the blood libel was strongest. Jews never talked about him and he was never mentioned by name – let alone Christ. He was known to us as Yoyzel (which actually implied the Crucifix), or more affectionately as Yosele Pandrok, Yishu of Nazareth. Father never mentioned his name but sometimes talked in an early Talmudic way of Oysch Hayish, literally Ecce Homo. And as we lived in a very Catholic country, we usually saw on the corners of a forest or at the cross-roads, a wooden figure of Christ dying on a Cross. My teacher warned me that passing the Cross with the figure of Christ Crucified, which was erected further down our street at the corner of the park, to be careful and hold on to my hat, so that the wind would not blow it off, and it might be taken that I am worshipping Christ by uncovering my head.

But when I quickly glanced with one eye while passing that little park corner, or even looked upon a church, and pretending to see him only by accident, my heart was full of sorrow for this crucified Jew whom the Goyim have captured and crucified him daily, as they murder daily his people – in his name – even now, and spread unimaginable calumnies, that we use Christian blood in our Matzos!

Of course, the reading of the New Testament was strictly forbidden in our homes, but from quotations in our history and bits and pieces here and there in controversial literature, we learned of certain writings and formed our own idea of the tragic story of Jesus, or Yishu Hanotzri – the Man of Nazareth.

When I first read the New Testament, I read it with fear and trembling. So many lies were there gathered together that it seemed too obvious that this book was an infamous accusation against the whole Jewish people. The New Testament was the Alpha and Omega of anti-Jewish literature. We had discovered the very source of anti-Semitism. When we read that Pontius Pilate asked the people in Jerusalem whom he should deliver to them – Jesus or Barabas – the crowd answered "Barabas". Crucify him! Crucify Jesus, and let his blood be on our heads!" This lie was such an obvious falsification of history, as if the same people who, only yesterday followed Jesus with Hosannahs and love, would now demand his crucifixion and ask for his blood to be on their heads!

No matter how little historical knowledge we had we knew from our sources, that Pontius Pilate was a murderously, cruel Procurator of Judea, a fierce enemy of the Jewish people and it's religion, and that no Pilate will ask the permission of a Jewish crowd, or it's servile priests to have him crucified, when the roads of Jerusalem were lined with hundreds (some say thousands) of crucified Jews. Even the most unhistorically minded person could see that this document i.e. (Mark), as the synoptic Gospels, including the anti-Jewish John wrote about a Century after the crucifixion of Jesus, were produced to placate the Roman people that Jesus was not crucified by the Roman Governor, but by the Jews themselves. But we knew from the Talmud that the Synhedrion had already lost the power to sentence anybody to death. We also knew something most significant from the Talmud, that a Synhedrion that delivered *one death sentence in seventy years*, was called a "Murderous Court". Not to mention the obvious historical fact that nailing a living person to the cross was a typical Roman capital punishment, leaving the victim there until he died. This was abhorred by the Jews as a most barbaric Roman method of killing, particularly Jewish rebels, the Zealots, against religious persecution and desecration of the Temple of Jerusalem.

I was drawn and, at the same time, repulsed by him. I loved and hated him at the same time. His words, we felt were distorted in the New Testament, so that the real Rabbi Jesus was hidden from us. He told Pharisees, that he didn't come to abolish the Law, but to fulfil it, and not one iota will he diminish from the Torah and it's commandments. And reading his words, we couldn't understand why we shouldn't love him.

But we knew nothing about him. Being a Chassid, I was not amazed at his miracles; we have heard about other Holy Rabbis, miracle workers, who drove out devils from mentally sick people.

CHAPTER ELEVEN

"From Childhood all the strength of my

Being had been devoted to the invention

of tales, plays and stories --thousands

of them. They lay on my heart like

toads on a stone. I was possessed by

a devilish pride and did not want to

write them down prematurely. I thought

it was a waste of time not to write as

well as Leo Tolstoy."

ISAAC BABEL

A t first I read, or had read to me, cheap novelettes and romances that were available in the local library, until one day I discovered real literature. Three of the great Yiddish writers were already dead and considered classics: Mendele Mochar Sforim, Peretz, Sholem Aleichem, and one was eagerly awaiting Sholem Asch's new novel. (Incidentally, Asch's novel "Kiddush Hashem" –

Hallowing the Name, is the only novel of all my young readings that made me cry).

I mentioned before that by accident I became a journalist on a local newspaper which a school friend of mine, Nata Goldkrantz (he perished, together with my relations and other colleagues in the Holocaust) was editing, before he was called up into the Polish Army service, for two years (a fate which I avoided by being disqualified as a soldier because of my imperfect health). After his call-up I became in his place, "editor". I tried to improve my page with articles on politics and literature, and with light essays which we called by the French word, feuilleton. I tried my best to give it a semblance of a big city paper, but the local gossip was so dull and boring that my articles, under half a dozen pseudonyms, tried to give some variety to the page, with a review on a new book, or a satirical essay on a local pompous worthy, who, I was told, was reading the sheet with interest.

I was also a contributor and co-editor of the *Socialist Live* Newspaper every Saturday evening, where I read articles on literature and famous writers, old and new, who celebrated their anniversaries or became topical.

A Story of Which Literature is Made

About that time a tragedy shook our town, which concerned me personally and intimately. There was a boy of about eighteen or nineteen years old whom I knew. I was working with him as a dentist's assistant. He was a flaxen haired Jewish orphan boy called Mietek, and he was staying with another dentist in town, Dr. Rothenberg, who brought him up, together with a girl of about the same age, Tosia, who was also an orphan and very beautiful, with magnificent black eyes and raven hair, which she wore in two big locks down her olive cheeks.

I frequently saw her in the street, going back with her books under her arm from school, or in the cinema on Sundays. The boy, Mietek, I knew, because I used to work with another dentist, Dr. Rothenberg's wife. The boy was terribly in love with Tosia and was following her everywhere she went.

One summer morning which promised to develop into a hot day, our telephone rang menacingly (it was the first telephone installed in our house a few weeks before), and a colleague of mine, Beno, was on the line and he said: "You've heard the news? Mietek Lejbushevitz shot Rothenberg's Tosia and himself. Weren't you in love with her yourself?"

This news hit me, as with a hammer. I threw down the receiver, and shouted – "I'm going right now!" I almost ran to town, over the bridge to the dentist's house. On a chestnut tree lined beautiful street, with fine houses, where the Bank was on the corner and the rich lived. I ran up the first flight of stairs, although there was a lift, and went into the house through the drawing-room, where there were a few people and two policemen. I opened the door to the bed-room, and saw Tosia's white bed with heavy, blood-stained cushions and sheets. A policeman stopped me and told me that nobody is allowed in the room, and that I mustn't touch anything. In another bedroom, at the end of the corridor, was the body of the boy Mietek. I couldn't see his face, it was covered up with a table cloth. I was told he had shot himself in the head which was in a terrible mess.

Dr. Rothenberg, the adopted father of this murdered couple, was walking up and down the darkened salon with its old-fashioned furniture, the chairs of a dark brocade. The curtains were not drawn and the big mirror opposite a seascape, was covered with a long white sheet, as it is customary in Jewish houses in mourning. Dr. Rothenberg's eyes were red-rimmed under his rimless glasses, and he was wiping the corners of his eyes with a silk handkerchief. He took off his glasses and put them on again in quick succession.

"Who could have imagined such a tragedy?" he said several times, as if talking to himself. I touched him on his shoulders as he sat in an arm chair; I couldn't find a word to say to him. "I went about seven o'clock in the morning for my walk, when Tosia unusually got up to go to school," he said quietly, looking at the picture with the golden frame on the wall. "I brought them up like brother and sister! Who would have imagined such an end?" he said and took off his glasses again.

People started coming in. The doctor had just left. School friends of Tosia's arrived, and two or three of her teachers.

They laid her out on the floor in a side room furnished with black lacquered Chinese furniture. She was covered with a black cover, and four silver candle-sticks were burning at her head.

It was Wednesday, and I was worried about my page in the newspaper, which was printed on Thursday in Piotrków, and distributed on Friday in our town. I usually sent the material with the driver of the omnibus which left daily with passengers. So, after a few words with the Commissioner of the Police, "To get the facts right", I asked Dr. Rothenberg's permission to use the dining-room to prepare the report, and I sat down by the table with pen and paper to write. For the first time in my life I was shocked at what I was doing, and as I wrote the first lines under the heading:

"TERRIBLE TRAGEDY IN OUR TOWN. MURDER AND SUICIDE OF TWO YOUNG LOVERS." – The door opened and Stefan Pawiewoki, the poet from Warsaw, who was a teacher in Tosia's Gymnasium, passed by (I had made his acquaintance a short time before), "You are writing a report?" he said, and I detected a shadow of irony in his question. And in a flash I was terribly ashamed of what I was doing – making journalistic reports of a ghastly tragedy, and I answered him with a quick, blatant lie: "No! No! I am writing something for Dr. Rothenberg; he asked me to do it for him!"

As he was a Pole and couldn't read Yiddish, I didn't bother to cover the page with the big headline. For the first time I was ashamed before a poet of journalism and reporting. I felt I am being callous and cynical to write about such a horrible tragedy, as if it were only material for a newspaper section, instead of writing a Romeo and Juliet.

But, subconsciously, I was not a little proud of my shame – to be a mere reporter of such a tragedy, and it seemed to be that the shame of my journalism deepened when passing the boy's room, and I noticed a book on the window-sill; I opened it, and I don't remember now whether I was surprised or not, when I saw that it had a glaring red title: Dostoyevsky's *Crime and Punishment*, almost as if I was expecting it, for I had only recently read this book, and I remember still the deep impression it made on me, and how I was fascinated and horrified by it, and read it lying in the sunny woods outside our town, on the Kaczka, where we had a "dacha", a peasant's hut, rented for the summer. And so, this was my first experience of being ashamed of journalism, which lasted in me for many of my growing years.

Amidst the school girls who came to the house to sit and mourn over the dead covered body of Tosia was also a girl of about eighteen called Adela. She went to the same school in the eighth class. It was this girl, Adela, whom I was in love with. Needless to say I thought she was very beautiful, and to describe her would be silly. She was a slim girl with a light complexion, blue eyes and honey-coloured hair. She looked to me more beautiful than any other woman I had ever seen, including Tosia who was lying murdered and covered on the floor, with whom I must have been slightly in love before I saw Adela.

When the funeral people came to take out the girl's body to the hearse, the school girls started a lament. Adela, too, broke out in tears, and I couldn't help crying myself. Suddenly the whole tragedy became deeply personal.

The street was full of mourners, all classes from the school with the teachers came to the funeral; on the hearse were masses of flowers in wreaths and the horses wore black covers. The funeral of the boy was not at the same time. Apparently the religious leaders ordered that they must not be buried at the same time.

His funeral took place late in the dark of the evening, and nobody except two or three relatives of the boy accompanied the burial. As a murderer and a suicide, he was not allowed to be buried in the Jewish cemetery, but outside behind the wall.

For weeks the whole town talked about nothing except this double tragedy. That such a shameful piteous deed should happen amongst their own people brought, perhaps, too many additional sorrows.

"A Jewish boy should do such a terrible thing!" some women said: "Is the end of the world" – sof welt. And, in fact, nobody had ever heard of a Jewish murder and suicide. This sort of thing one heard only about the Goyim, who murdered one another – and particularly Jews …

For weeks I couldn't pass the house of Dr. Rothenberg without thinking of this terrible tragedy. I began to imagine that I had loved her more than in reality I really had – more even than Adela. After all it was such a romantic tragedy about which I read in some book. In my heart I blamed all the romantic poets and writers who have, since Shakespeare and Goethe, suggested such subjects. In my naïvety I even blamed Dostoyevsky for this double crime. But I also thought that when life imitates literature it is always in the worst taste.

A few weeks later, passing one afternoon in the market place, I saw Dr. Rothenberg sitting beside a young girl in an open droshka. She was quite pretty, in mourning dress, holding a bunch of flowers in her lap. This was the sister of the murdered girl, I was told by a woman who was standing by the Kosceszko Statue. He brought her down to stay with him in his house. The whole scene was tragic-comic, and it looked like a stupid happy ending in a very bad film. They were riding out to the cemetery.

CHAPTER TWELVE

For weeks and months this tragedy was the talk of the town. What really happened? Did she reject him completely? Did he try to rape her? The Police inquiry said that nothing had been found to make them believe that. There were no letters, no notes left. Though they lived in the same house, nobody had ever seen them together in the street. Nobody suspected the slightest love affair. I knew the boy better than anybody else because I worked with him in the dentist's laboratory. He was not a bad looking boy, with light brown hair and grey-blue eyes. He had a pale face and tightly drawn lips. Nobody would have thought that he could hold a revolver in his boney hands. He was withdrawn, polite, and rarely spoke except when you addressed him. Who would fathom such a double tragedy?

After a few months the whole terrible affair was forgotten, and some people, seeing Dr. Rothenberg with her sister (she must have been a year or two older than Tosia and not so pretty), together with the flowers in the droshka going to the cemetery, wondered if he will now marry her …

I busied myself indiscriminately and voraciously with so called great books. It was this time when I fell under the spell of Oscar Wilde, in translation of course. What made me a convert to Wilde were three things; his wit, his dandyism, and in particular a little book of his called *Man's Soul Under Socialism*. I was greatly impressed by his *Portrait of Dorian Gray*, which made a special impact on me.

My first great guide into European literature, and particularly the romantics of the nineteenth century, was the great Jewish Dane

Georg Brandes, the most famous critic in Europe at the time, now almost forgotten.

But to return to Oscar Wilde, whose *Ballad of Reading Gaol*, moved me deeply. Books from Germany and literary magazines, as well as the revolutionary poets and writers of Russia which were then most popular in Poland, had a great influence on us, and Mayakovksy, Blok and Yesenin, were widely read. After reading some Left German and Russian magazines, mostly violent propaganda against British Imperialism, I came to the conclusion that Oscar Wilde was a victim of this pernicious Imperialism and hypocrisy and the exploitation of the toiling masses round the world that was coloured pink on the maps, and that the Russian Revolution, after reading *Ten Days That Shook The World*, by an enthusiastic American, will free the world of all exploiters and human misery. And we, the young generation, believed in it absolutely.

I joined a literary and musical society called HaZamir, and there I was invited, or invited myself, to give a lecture. Various subjects were suggested but I had chosen an original subject which I was sure nobody in town knew anything about, and I considered myself an expert on it, and for a peculiar moral reason: The moral reason was that I felt myself strongly influenced by the tragic figure of Oscar Wilde. I became a Socialist by reading *Man's Soul under a Socialist Society*. Another affinity with the author of the *Portrait of Dorian Gray*, was rather unusual.

I had lost my virginity about that time. An older colleague had taken me to a woman who, long past her youth, lived in a small cottage in the back streets behind the fields, and there she received "visitors". After this memorable visit to her I had such a repulsion to myself and felt such deep shame, that I remember looking at myself for long stretches of time into the big wall mirror to see how ugly I was getting – from minute to minute. Like the Portrait of Dorian Gray I felt myself getting horribly old and ugly and my face, which I had always thought in my vanity to be delicate and not unpleasant, seemed to be getting an ugliness which was spreading over my pale face from minute to minute. In the morning it seemed to me that I had become still more repulsive and that at any moment my face will be covered in deep pock marks. The most extraordinary feeling was that I had betrayed the girl I loved, Adela. It somehow had nothing to do with her …but I had betrayed Love itself, for the thought of ever making love to Adela never entered my mind. What I wanted was only to hold her hands, and perhaps kiss her. They were two quite different things; one was love that I read about in novels, the other was immoral desires and wild passions of the flesh to which I had recently awakened. They seemed to have nothing whatsoever to do with each other. One was something sacred and the other something very profane. For the feeling of unrequited Heavenly love of which there was nothing earthly, Adela was as much responsible as my own immaturity. When I was once with her alone in the room and she was turned with her back to me, I approached her stealthily and put my lips to her exposed neck. She turned like a frightened cat and cried in Polish one word: "Swinia" – Pig.

Maybe she was right, perhaps it is a swinish thing to do to a girl that you love so much? Perhaps dreaming of her and gazing stealthily was enough? I had also waking dreams of glory about her; dreams that only a boy of sixteen can have … . She had fallen into a river that divided our town, by the market, and she is drowning … and I, passing the bridge, jump into the river from the height of the wooden bridge, and I rescue her! And her father, the history teacher Sanina, praises me in joy and says that I may marry her! But as for carnal relations, of which I had only recently had the first taste, that was too awful and too disgusting to contemplate.

It was then that I read *Dorian Gray*, and I kept looking in the mirror to see how my face changes into a horrible mask of an old, ugly lecher or, as Adela said, a swine. And so I changed almost over night from a little Jewish Hamlet into a repulsive sinner and lecher.

While I was constantly thinking of the author of *Dorian Gray*, I informed the Committee of the club that my lecture will be on Oscar Wilde. Besides the already mentioned books of Oscar Wilde, I knew only *Lady Windermere's Fan*, *The Importance of Being Ernest*, and *Salome*, and a German book on Wilde, together with some odd articles. About the real, unfortunate Oscar Wilde, and the subsequent notorious scandal which became the cause celebre towards the end of the Century, and which shook Europe, I knew next to nothing. It was obvious to me, as to any sensible man, that the whole thing was nothing but a gigantic frame-up by the Conservative leaders of Imperialist England, who wanted to compromise Wilde for his aesthetic socialism. It was obviously a lie because who would believe that so witty and elegant a genius and dandy, the arbeiter elegantarium of fashionable England's salons, whom thousands of beautiful women must have loved, and were ready to give him their love, would be a homosexual? Frankly I didn't know what homosexuality was except for a naïve vague idea mentioned darkly in the Talmud and in the Bible. For what man in his senses will have any sexual leaning for a man when there are so many beautiful women in the world?

And so I delivered my lecture before an interested audience, proving, with this argument, the impossibility of Wilde's homosexuality, and that the whole scandal was staged by the black reactionaries of England that hunted out this great genius first in to prison, and then abroad. The lecture didn't go off badly, in spite of a terrible misfortune I had near the beginning of the lecture, which I was reading from narrow sheets of paper, and, turning from page 9 – I came to page 26! I was confused for a moment or two, looking for page 10, but hitting on page 15, with super-human courage, I bravely continued the lecture by heart — as a man who can't swim when on the point of drowning. Nobody noticed the difference. There was applause after I finished, and some acquaintances and friends came over to congratulate me, and actually agreed with my fantastic theory.

Since that first lecture I have never again used written papers, even when I do make notes I usually forget to look at them.

That my lecture on poor Oscar Wilde, the cruel victim of British reactionary Lords of the High Courts, was approved of I also knew from the fact that another lecture, this time on Anatole France, was arranged for me.

My lectures and articles spoken on the *living* newspaper and printed in the provincial weekly gave me a certain notoriety in town. "(*Living* meant that the various contributors not only *printed* their articles, but also read them aloud from the platform to audiences).

I was spoken of as an Apikores, or epicurean, which means in

Yiddish an Atheist or non-believer and socialist. I read unceasingly, and started to write some serious pieces, and so called poems.

One day I wrote down a prose poem, which I thought was the best I had ever written. It was a poem about Jesus and how he came to Granada and is there taken by the Inquisition to prison, together with other Jews. The Inquisitor orders Jesus to be tortured and asks him to admit that he is a Morano, and that he should proclaim himself a true Christian and believer in the Holy Trinity. And to save his soul, they burn him on the auto-da-fé, and Jesus dies with the words: "Eli, Eli, lama Azavtoni", and not "Lomo Sabactani" – which is Aramaic, as the New Testament has it.

Some time later I happened to read Dostoyevsky's *The Brothers Karamazov* which impressed me infinitely more than *Crime and Punishment*, but when I came to the famous chapter about the *Grand Inquisitor*, in which Jesus is brought to the Inquisitor, just like in my poem, but *not* because he was a Jew but because he brought freedom to Man, and the Inquisitor tells Jesus not to interfere with the Church and teach people love and freedom. What Man needs is Authority … And Jesus remains silent to all the ravings of the Inquisitor.

Though I realised immediately that Dostoyevsky's *Grand Inquisitor* was infinitely more profound and more and more beautiful than my badly written piece, I was ashamedly and secretly convinced that my prose poem was truer. Imagine, therefore, how I felt some months later when a book by Georg Brandes (who was my Cicerons in European literature) fell into my hands. The book was called simply "*Russia*", after a journey he had made there, in which I found a note that in a first version of the *Grand Inquisitor*, Dostoyevsky had Jesus burned by the Inquisition on the auto-da-fé, just like in my fantasy.

No matter how conscious of my failings and modest I may have been, and overwhelmed by Dostoyevsky's terrifying genius, I couldn't help feeling a tiny ray of pride breaking into my heart, that he and I have chosen the same subject.

And though I needed no explanation that Dostoyevsky's story was infinitely more profound than my story, there was, I thought, a tremendous difference in the conception; my Jesus was a Jewish Christ and he dies a Jewish death – a Morano at the stake.

CHAPTER THIRTEEN

For weeks and months afterwards this accidental affinity with the great tormented Dostoyevsky made me incapable of writing anything serious. It must have had a demoralising effect on me: You see, demonic Dostoyevsky's mind worked on the same lines as my own. I am afraid that this was not inducive to modesty. Though I perfectly realized his grandeur, and his anti-Catholic sweep, which I appreciated and applauded, and his overwhelming literary and artistic superiority, I, nevertheless, couldn't help myself but feeling somewhat secretly proud of my poorly written, but deeply felt, prose poem.

I haven't seen this piece of writing in all these years … together with other attempts, I destroyed it years ago. But what remained in my heart and mind since then was the hatred for the lies and hypocrisy of the Church and a tormenting love for the Crucified One. For the first time I began secretly to read the New Testament, and I was horrified by many viciously anti-Jewish statements.

Most of the Jews, I learned with great amazement, knew nothing about Jesus – or as much as the Christians knew about the Jews at the time of Jesus.

We knew that the Talmud had anti-Christian and derogatory passages about Yisha Patera and the Minim (as we called the sect of Christians) were always spoken of with contempt and changed into *Malshinim*, meaning denouncers, but we couldn't see anything new in the teaching of Jesus, except him being a follower of the prophet Amos, the first prophet of Love, and the saintly Rabbi Hillel, who lived some fifty years before Jesus. In our hearts we knew that we couldn't have condemned Jesus to the Cross for two weighty reasons:

The Jews in Judea, being Roman occupied territory, had no power to commit anybody to death, and Crucifixion was definitely a Roman capital punishment.

I am trying to write this without hind-knowledge of the historical material and documentation that I have read since that time by Christian and Jewish scholars, in hundreds of books and learned articles. I try to write this with the very limited knowledge I had at that early age, and the very superficial guess work and, perhaps, very intuitive understanding of a boy only fifteen to sixteen years of age when I first looked into the New Testament and came to the conclusion that, with all its beautiful, ethical passages, which reminded me of the Bible, as, for instance: "Love thy neighbour as Thyself." And the greatest commandment of all is: "Thou shalt love thy God with all your heart and with all your soul and with all your might", – and in spite of the admonition of Jesus *not* to go to the Gentiles, and that he came only to the lost sheep of his people Israel, or "The Salvation is of the Jews", I nevertheless saw in that book the origin of Jew hatred and the whole teaching of anti-Semitism. I saw right away the tendency to white-wash Pontius Pilate and burden the whole Jewish people with the crime of the Crucifixion, and make the Romans just tools in the hands of the Jews, when every Jew with the slightest knowledge of history knew that Pilate had crucified hundreds of Jewish rebels and zealots on the roads of Judea, as the Jewish historian, (proud of being a Jew, but an admirer of the Romans) Josephus, had testified.

Here and there I read a life of Jesus, or a History of Christianity, of the Church Fathers, and every time I was horrified by the savage hatred for Judaists in the New Testament and the exegeses. Even the enlightened great scholar Renan in his life of Jesus, which was put on the index by the Catholic Church, makes Jews completely responsible for the Crucifixion.

One day I read a Jewish translation of a book called *Toldoth Yishu*, which was probably written in the Middle Ages, during the Crusades, which documented whole Jewish towns in Germany on the way to liberate Jerusalem from the Muslims and Jews. It was a scurrilous, stupid and obscene pamphlet, probably by a Jew out of his mind and writing, in revenge, about Jesus almost in the same language as the

Christians wrote about the Jews for innumerable centuries in His Name. This is the only Jewish book that I was ever ashamed of. It was more stupid than evil. As a blasphemous book it was not passed by the censors or sold openly, or kept in any library, you could only lay hands on it in the underground – on the, so-called, blackest market.

I was ashamed of this silly and mendacious book. No matter how little I knew of history, and how ignorant I was in canonical writing, I asked myself: What has the sublime prophet Jesus got to do in any way with the Church? A great curiosity had driven me to find out more about Christianity.

What do they do in the Church?

On one Christmas Eve, I borrowed a suit from a Polish colleague who lived not far from us and, disguised as a Polish boy, I stole myself into the big Catholic Church of St. Anthony for the midnight service. I stood squashed between the crowd of men and women, mostly peasant folk who smelled of the earth and cow dung. Nobody had any prayer books and neither did I. The priest stood at the corner on a pedestal, dressed in white, and gave the sermon. There were a lot of Polish words and Latin, which I couldn't understand. I wondered whether the crowd of country peasants could understand any better than I.

It was all strange, and mysterious and beautiful I thought, and yet I was afraid of being discovered: A Jew who came to mock at the holiest Christian Service! But I didn't come to mock, I came to experience with my own eyes the mystery. In my nostrils was the smell of peasant women's bodies; it was an intoxicating smell of hay and fields mixed with cheap perfumed soap. By the Western wall on an altar was a crib with a little babe Jesus in painted wood, dressed in torn up, but clean, linen, under a broken roof, with two wooden cows standing amidst freshly laid straw and hay. I was pressed towards two girls in their coloured, national peasant dresses, and I could feel their buttocks and their legs next to my body. The girls had pink cheeks and white bodies, with many strings of coloured glass beads with a little cross in the middle. They had coloured scarves on their heads. The warmth of the bodies and the heat of the burning big candles gave out a strong smell, acrid and pleasant.

And all this for the birth of a Jewish boy – two thousand years ago? I was both amazed and afraid of my own courage. What if they discover me and say I came to stab and desecrate the Host, which Jews were always accused of? I, on the contrary, was afraid that the priest, in his gold and silver vestments, will produce from under the table a Jewish child – perhaps a boy of my own age, if not myself – and slaughter me on the Alter, as one slaughters a lamb – a lamb like the Lamb under the Cross, painted on the wall and hung by the side of a Cross with a long, pale, crucified Christ and mysterious letters in three scripts, Hebrew, Latin and Greek. These ominous letters which mean (as it was later explained to me), "Jesus Nazaretus Rex Iudeorum, King of the Jews." I looked at the paintings on the walls with pictures of saints, whose names I didn't know, among whom I recognized only one, St. Paul. Him I recognized as I had seen, in a friend's house, a painting of St. Paul with his dark, threatening beard. It was a twin portrait by Durer on the cover of a book of Art History, (probably the first picture I ever saw which impressed me deeply) but I couldn't distinguish which is St. Peter and which St. Paul. They both had long beards, but Paul's beard was more sinister and darker.

The incense tickled my nose. Is this the same Ktoires which the High Priest used in the Sanctuary of the Temple, about which I read so much in the Bible and Talmud?

I was suffocating from the heat of the peasant's bodies, and the pungent smell of the incense and the candles. What is a Jewish boy doing here in *Boze Narodzienie*, the birth of the Christian God? Couldn't it be taken, if I were discovered, as a dangerous provocation? A Talmud Jew, whose ancestors crucified Christ, here in Catholic Church of St. Anthony?

The fat priest was saying the prayers in Latin and then gave his sermon in Polish. And, the most extraordinary thing, this priest with the light purple face and many red little veins on his nose, and flabby cheeks (I stood almost opposite him), didn't say a word that the Jews crucified Jesus, or that the Jews kill Christian children for their Passover. Not a word. And from all the history I have read I was told that not a sermon was told by priests without mentioning the crimes and sufferings, and humiliations that the Jews caused Jesus, and that they are being punished to this day for deicide, and are doomed to eternal persecution. But what am I doing here? What will I say if I am asked what has a Jewish boy to do in a Catholic Church on Christmas Eve? Did I come to mock them? To spy on them? Was I sent by the Komuno-Kahal, the secret Jewish society which works for the conquest of the World? Although I was squashed between peasant women and men and young boys and girls, was hot, and could hardly breathe, my heart was beating fast and my mouth was dry with fear.

Will they believe me if I'll tell them that my terrible curiosity about Jesus, and what they have done to a healing Jewish Rabbi, had brought me here?

The crowd started leaving through the big door at the end of the Church. Hiding my face with my elbow as well as I could, I squeezed myself to the exit and was swallowed by the crowd outside. It was snowing gently, and it was not cold. I put on my Polish cap and went home, over the bridge which divided our town.

In our courtyard I went into the wood shed by the water pump, where I had left my Jewish black gabardine and round Jewish black cloth cap. I was afraid to bring home the Gentile, or as they were called German, clothes, and which I was then starting to wear clandestinely, so that my uncle and aunt shouldn't notice them. This was a daring thing to do, for we Jews, the old and the young, were always dressed in these long dark grey Yolitza, a sort of split garbardine reaching to our ankles, a dress that had been worn, by Jews only, since the Middle Ages. My earlocks, which I had worn since I was a boy of five years, were already cut by the hairdresser, and I began to grow my hair. This was the beginning of my determination to become Europeanised.

. . . .

"Oh! God★ I could be bounded in a

nutshell and count myself a King of

infinite space, were it not that I

have bad dreams.

HAMLET.

100

Since my childhood I have been suffering from bad dreams and nightmares, some of them were re-current with many variations.

One of the dreams that occurred quite often to me (and, for the first time on that night of the Christmas Eve visit to Midnight Mass) was that I stood amongst a huge, wailing and excited crowd somewhere on a hill in Jerusalem. I push myself through the crowd, interspersed with Roman soldiers and legionnaires, who look like Cossacks but wear magnificent uniforms, to the top of the hill with the three crosses, on which three men are hanging. In the middle was Jesus, his loins wrapped in a Tallith with four fringes at the corner. It looked just like my fathers' Sabbath Tallith, only without the head piece of braided silver thread. On the top of the Cross I can make out some writing in three languages, the Hebrew and the Latin I can read, the Greek I cannot. But it must obviously mean the same: Isu Hanotzri Melech Yehudim, Jesus Nazaretus Rex Indeorum. I stand underneath the Cross and, as I am trying to lift my head and look at the face of Jesus, distorted by agony with white foam and blood dribbling down his reddish small beard, a drop of blood falls on my cheek. I try to shout and scream, but I cannot get a sound out of my mouth.

At that moment a Roman legionary with a metal helmet and armour, takes out a broad sword from his sheath, and gives me a wallop with the broad-side of the sword on my shoulder, which hurts terribly. I try again to scream, but I can't get out a sound, and I wake up, soaked in cold sweat.

Other frightening dreams were more common: The falling dreams from Heaven; the dream that I have to run from a dangerous man with a knife, and I can't lift my feet. I am escaping from fire, and the fire envelopes me and I am nearly burned. I am drowning in the river whilst trying to swim, but I am drowning – I swallow water and it chokes me. These last two kinds of dreams were memories of reality: A few years ago, when I was about eleven, I was bathing with a colleague of mine. He was a good swimmer and I was not, although my father, who was himself a remarkable swimmer, tried to teach me, because it is written somewhere in the Holy Books that a father should teach his son to swim as early as possible, so that he could save the life of someone drowning. My colleague saved my life that day, and held me up, only putting my head under the water every time I tried to struggle with my arms and feet, to calm down my desperate struggling. He held me up by my hair and ducked me many times. He dragged me out to the high shore, on to a patch of grass, and he was trying to squeeze my belly to see that I had not swallowed too much water. I was lucky not to have swallowed too much water, and lying on my back, I looked up to the blue sky. A Polish peasant passed by and I remember asking him in my halting Polish: "Panie, czy bede Zyt?" – "Will I live?"

I nearly died another death by fire. And the thought that I could have been murdered at the same time when my father was killed, never left my mind or my re-current dreams at night.

But the escape from being burned alive made a shattering impression on me. It happened on a Saturday evening. We had then an elderly poor woman staying with us, as a help in the kitchen of my aunt, (who moved in with her husband into my house and were made my guardians by the Court). The maid, Gitel, was the widow of a poor tailor, who was left with a grown son, Velvel, who, one day, went out of his mind and started threatening her with a big pair of scissors. She, herself, Gitel, was "not all there", she would be frightened to death by the slightest accident in the kitchen, such as a pot boiling over on the stove, or a hot burning coal falling from the fire on to the floor. I remember her once, when the Polish woman Yadwiga, the wife of the caretaker Kozarek, who was climbing up on a chair to light the high gas lamp near the ceiling, screaming that she wont stay in the house because if Yadwiga will fall down and kill herself, people will say that "the Jews killed her for Passover", and she ran out into the courtyard. It was she who went to the shop to fill up the oil lamp from a huge metal barrel of naptha which stood in the corner. Like the fool she was, she came in with the lamp in her hands, and screwing off the glass and wick, she filled the lamp while the wick was still alight. The whole barrel of oil caught light and burst out into a huge flame. It was Saturday evening, just as it was getting dark, and my aunt was finishing her prayers, which are said at the close of the Sabbath before a star appears in the sky. I was lying on the sofa and I put away the book I was reading when I saw the flames. I heard a terrific explosion, and I ran into the shop and stood on the other side of the door, not knowing what to do. At the same time my aunt caught the bedding from the bed and threw it on to the burning barrel of oil. The flames were squashed for a second, but at the same time she noticed her coat sticking out from the top of the barrel. She pulled out the already burning coat from under the bedding to try to save it, but the whole feather bedding came out as well, and the huge flames were blocking my way back into the room where the other door was which led into the street. It was locked with an iron bar. And there I was between the flaming floor and barrel! With unprecedented courage, I jumped over the flames, but as I did so my own coat caught fire and began to burn. Somebody threw a sack over my back which smothered and put out the flames. Thus I escaped a certain death by fire. My aunt screamed in the corridor for the neighbours to help, and people started running in with buckets of water.

Outside the fire brigade arrived with their primitive water wagons and ladders. The whole shop and sitting room were enveloped in flames.

From the Prayer House arrived a number of Jews, my father's Chassidim, who ran in to help. But a few of them, the more pious, began to throw the collection of books from my shelves in to fire, saying that, because of these Godless, unclean treyfus books, the fire struck after the murder of my father and the death of my mother, so as to teach me a lesson.

I never hated the Chassidim more, and flaunted my Godlessness and epicureanism to spite them.

The house was saved, but almost my whole library was thrown into the flames wilfully by these Chassidic fanatics. The shop with most of it's "colonial products", tea, sugar, spices, chocolate, rice, coffee, tobacco and cigarettes, were burned. The whole shop was destroyed. Everybody was praising my courage, how I jumped over the flames – otherwise I might have become a "living torch!"

I was furious about the Chassidim burning my books, and was looking for some revenge. I couldn't have been more "Godless" than I was. So I started smoking, and I smoked on the Sabbath, naturally not in the street, but locked in my room or in the outside toilet, or at a friend's house, who was also a free thinker and a non-believer.

I wrote on the Sabbath and cleaned my shoes with black polish – even in front of my aunt, who threatened me that, not only will I burn in Hell (the fire was obviously just a warning!) but the soul of my father and mother will be expelled from Heaven for my sins.

My plan of revenge on the Chassidim was, I thought, rather worth making:

The Sefer Torah, the Holy Scroll of the Five Books of Moses which my father had had written especially for me and was, like my house and shop, part of my inheritance, was being kept in the Prayer House, together with other pure parchment Torahs, some ancient ones, a century or two old.

I approached the President of the community and told him that I wanted the return of the Scroll with the silver crown and silver "hand" (the pointer which is used while reading aloud the section of the week, on every Sabbath, and on Mondays and Thursdays, besides all the usual holidays). I waited several weeks and no answer arrived from them. I decided then not to wait any longer, and somehow literally "took the Law into my own hands."

On a hot summer afternoon I broke into the Synagogue when there was nobody there, unlocked the *Oron Kodesh*, the Holy Shrine, and took out my Torah from the Shrine, which stood among several others, to the writing of which father had also contributed. I wrapped it around with a black edged Tallith that was lying there, and, running through the wild fields at the back of the Prayer House into the Gentile part of the town, I brought up the Torah to a friend of ours, a mathematics teacher, whom I knew I could trust. A colleague of mine, Moshe, helped me in this act of "vengeance" on the Chassidim who had burned my books. We put it into a cupboard of which we had the key.

The next morning, which was a Monday, the news spread that I had committed the ultimate blasphemy, stealing the Holy Scroll where it is plainly written – "Thou shalt not steal."

Most of the Jews condemned me, but there were some, the progressives, the *maskilim*, and the socialist unbelievers, who were on my side, and said that the Torah belonged, legally to me, the son and heir, and that you can't steal your own property, even if it is so Holy a property as a Torah.

The only thing to remember is that the Holy Scroll must be guarded carefully and must be carried like a child to one's breast, and you must be careful not to drop it – God forbid! Neither must you have it in a bedroom where people have carnal relations with their wives.

The Jews of the Chassidic Prayer House threatened me with the Police, and the Law Courts if I didn't return it within twenty-four hours. They threatened to put me in Hairem, i.e. excommunicating me from the Jewish community, which meant that nobody must have anything to do with me, or speak to me, or have me in their homes, or stand within four yards of me; the worst and most dreaded punishment that the Rabbinical Court had power to inflict on me a "Public Sinner". This threat intrigued me more than anything else that could befall me. I shall be put in Hairem like the glorious Spinoza, who was my exalted and spiritual guide – though I still couldn't understand him properly. Spinoza and a distant relation of his, Uriel da Costa, also a philosopher and dangerous heretic who was driven to suicide after his Hairem. On my desk I had a copy of a painting of Da Costa and the young boy Spinoza, studying together from a big book. There was another painting on my desk, a dark picture of Spinoza as he was attacked by a religious fanatic with a knife and nearly stabbed to death. The very idea of me and Spinoza and Da Costa fighting fanaticism and religious bigotry, gave me cause to be not a little proud of myself, and convincing myself that I am a modern philosopher and European humanist in the making.

Europe, the European man, the good European, these were our ideals, because I was convinced that I was born in the Middle Ages, and only in 1920 did I realise that I lived in the twentieth century. Nineteen Nineteen, I thought, was still the nineteenth century.

And, of course, Socialism was our greatest hope, so inspired were we by the Russian Revolution. For "Tomorrow" – next year – the Revolution will spread to Poland, to Germany, to France – to the whole of Europe – and, perhaps, to America too.

But in the late twenties, two or three years after Lenin's death, I began to get inside information about the Bolsheviks from a young

Communist, whose father was a friend of mine, and I used to visit his house almost every evening, play chess, drink wine-coloured Russian tea, which was even nicer without lemon. I had heard that the tea could also be drunk with milk – English fashion, which was called "Herbata po Angielsku", it had a strange taste, rather exotic, but I liked the idea. Having drunk such a glass with milk and sugar, I slowly began to feel I was an Englishman. But how does an Englishman feel? How does he behave? How does he act? We heard a lot of bad things against British Imperialism. There was India. There was oil in Persia; there was the Middle East. And there was such a case as Oscar Wilde, a victim of British hypocrisy, and later Bernard Shaw making fun of the British – good-naturedly. We only knew the myth of an England; a far away island, on top of Europe to the North on the map of the World, most of it pink … all British possessions, colonies, protectorates, and the British Empire. We knew that the Whites are exploiting the Blacks and the Yellow races; We knew the caricature of John Bull with top hat and flag, we knew the Englishman Sherlock Holmes, cap and pipe (which I tried to imitate), and we knew, in our town, one man, young and elegant, English fashion, whom we called the Prince of Wales. Actually a man called Henry Landsberg, the son of the biggest cloth manufacturer, whose worsted cloth, it was said, equalled the best of English woollens, and was exported abroad. He was the model of the Englishman – tall, good-looking, a fine face and slim figure. He dressed in the latest English fashion, including a "Boater" and white flannels, with a blue jacket in the summer for tennis. He used to ride through town in a carriage and pair with his mother and sister. His mother was middle aged and still had a handsome face and must have been beautiful in her youth. The face of the young sister, a girl about eighteen or twenty, was rather ordinary.

They drove through the town like royalty, and people passing on the pavement would raise their hats to them. They were known as the first rich aristocratic family in town, who actually lived in a Palace, which stood in the gardens of a side street not far from their factories. Whenever I used to pass the street, I marvelled at the high iron fence and huge gates, and gazed at the palace – a sort of structure that I knew only from illustrations in old novels.

CHAPTER FOURTEEN

At that time I began to dream a boyish fantasy that I will discover one day somebody who would discover me. I had, as is usual with young men of my environment and my reading, particularly after the death of my father and my mother, an exaggerated idea of my hidden talents, which needed only someone with a sympathetic mind and good eyes, to reveal to the world my genius. I didn't think of myself as ugly, I had rather a pleasant face, I thought, with questioning black eyes, a small nose, slightly more upturned than Jewish, and black curling hair – now that I had, in defiance of the religious law, had my long black earlocks cut off by the barber, which, together with my short German jacket and brown hat, made me look, I thought, completely European. Still I was not satisfied with my looks and tried various white collars, stiff and soft ones, with a variety of ties, which I started buying (to wear even a black tie was considered very advanced), and rounded collars with white fronts and stiff detachable cuffs.

And, got up like this, and sometimes even without a hat, I looked like some provincial amateur actor. As I paraded in these clothes I thought I heard Jews who knew me saying under their breath … "There goes the young fellow who stole the Sefer Torah (not *his* Sefer Torah)", and pointed their fingers at me. Father's Chassidim didn't stop bemoaning my fate that I, the only son of Reb Elia, who was prayed for for so many years by many Rabbis, should grow up into a Godless Meshumed and Apikores, worse than a Goy, for a Goy at least believes in *something* …

And I have even heard when father was alive that it is written in the

Holy Books, that if you travel with a peasant and he doesn't take off his cap when passing a crucifix, you may be in danger of your life …

The battle with the Chassidim and the President of the Prayer House went on for months. I wouldn't tell a soul where I had hidden the Sefer Torah (only three people, my friend Mosheh and the mathematics teacher, Balaban and I, myself, knew of it's hiding place in the cupboard).

Finally, after many threats and delegations sent to talk to me – whether I realize that it is "desecrating" such a Holy book as a Sefer Torah, and that it may bring misfortune not only to me, but to the whole Jewish community in town, and to my saintly parents, (blessed be their names), that they might even be expelled from Paradise, and I might be condemned to the eternal fires of Hell..

I replied that I'd take the risk! And, calmly, like the philosopher I imagined myself to be, I asked them in return if it is not a sin to deprive an orphan, as the only heir, of his rightful property?

After long drawn out "negotiations" with the notables of the Prayer House and a good deal of heckling, I was paid a sum of several hundred zlotys, the equivalent of about £200 or more, which was a considerable amount of money, and which I spent, in defiance of the fanatics who burnt my books, on buying other Godless books and dangerous literature, the reading of which could make you a free-thinker or a goy.

The truth was though that I had a mystical love for the Jewish people and it's martyrs history, I thought Jewish religion a terrible burden, especially on the young: The hundreds of "don'ts" and tabus (there are a Tariag Mitzvehs – or six hundred and thirteen commandments of "dos" and "don'ts" in our religion, and only a Tzadik, a Holy man, can fulfil them all). I decided that it is too difficult to be a Tzadik, as it is even too hard to be a Jew, as the proverbial folklore has it. I wanted to be as free as a Goy, but not lose my spiritual Jewishness. There was something unique in Jewish history; no other people in the whole world survived such suffering as we did in Egypt. What happened to Babylon, to Persia, Assyria, or even the great Hellenes and the mighty Romans? They remained in their own soil, their States were not abolished. We were not allowed

Camille, 1914, Poland.

*Camille with his mother,
Sura, 1915.*

*Camille outside the British
Museum, 1932.*

Above: Pat, 1933.

Right: Pat on the way to Australia on the SS Mariposa, *1940.*

Pat and Camille, Port Said, 1940.

Allegra and Camille, U.K., 1942.

Above: Camille with Yehudi, Allegra and Zuleika, New York, 1947.
Top right: Allegra, Zuleika, Pat, Yehudi and Camille Sao Paulo Brazil 1953.
Bottom right: Camille, Jaffa, Israel, 1967.

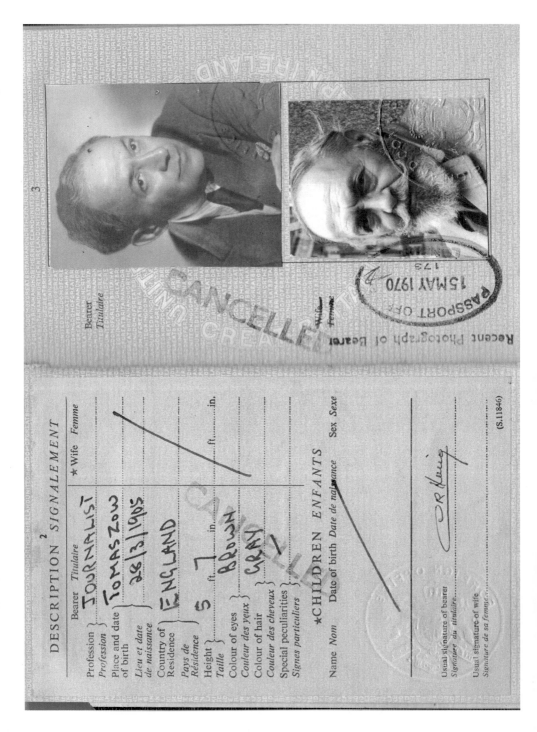

Camille's passport.

to remain on our soil in Judea. We went into exile, into the diaspora. God knows what might have happened to us had we remained in our Native land. We would have played such an important part in the history of mankind as Modern Iraq or Syria! And where have the ancient Greeks and Romans disappeared to? The present day Greeks and Italians, so historians say, have very little to do with the ancient Romans and Hellenes.

The further I went away from religion and religious practices, the more devoted I became to that inexplicable feeling of Jewishness which I could combine with my Europeanism. It was not Jewish nationalism, which is as bad as any other nationalism.

My Jewishness was a kind of Universalism and cosmopolitanism, or intellectualism, which was the hallmark of Socialism. About Zionism I was rather sceptical, although I admired Herzl and loved the idea of a Jewish Land – Eretz Israel – which is in every young Jewish heart, enveloped in holiness and in legend. I read in the Talmud that even the air of the land of Israel makes one wise.

There was a time when I even wanted to go myself as a pioneer to Palestine, and I even went so far as to go to Warsaw and visited, without an appointment, a famous Jewish mystical writer, Hillel Zeitlin, who was suspect with the ultra-orthodox Chassidim, and asked him whether I should go to Palestine. He was sitting with an open volume of the Talmud. He answered me laconically: "No, you will be torn out by the roots".

I didn't know then that he himself had two young sons working on a Kibbutz in Palestine, who were living in great hardship. One of them, Aaron Zeitlin, whom I knew later in Warsaw, became one of the foremost Jewish poets. Old Hillel Zeitlin, Aaron's brother, and his whole family were to perish in the Warsaw Ghetto under the Germans. Aaron Zeitlin was saved to a wretched survival in New York because he was, at the outbreak of the war, on a visit to the States.

I was nearer the Socialist Bund, the majority party of the Jewish workers, but I had never been an actual member of the Party. All Parties were mass movements from which I, as an individual, felt myself excluded.

So, I grew up a Jewish Socialist, and was flattered to be admired by the working classes, who were exploited, poor, and hungry, who saw that I, the son of a most pious Chassidic wealthy home, should join the Revolutionary class, rather than the bourgeoisie. I steeped myself in the Revolutionary memoirs of the Russian and Jewish social democrats, and, as I saw in the Nationalism, the source of all wars and ills of mankind, I thought that Zionism will not solve the Jewish problem, and that only Socialism will do away with the evil of anti-Semitism. And Socialism is coming tomorrow, or the day after, and it will come from Russia, where Jews had suffered most from oppression and pogroms, but are now free and equal – and anti-Semitic slogans (even denigrating "Zyd" (Yid), was forbidden to be used, and changed into the softer word "Yevrey".

We were convinced that the new Messiah will come from Russia! And there will be freedom, equality and happiness for the whole world. And there will be, above all, no more Jew hatred, no more killings and persecutions, and anti-Semitism will be a forgotten plague.

This hope, these dreams, were part of my Socialism and Europeanism. I was interested in every literature of Europe. I read the foreign press. I was the only reader in town, probably, of a variety of good German magazines: *Die Weltbuchen* and *Das Tagebuch*, I subscribed to an informative weekly, *Die Literasche Welt*.

I read incessantly, day and night. I carried, proudly, a book under my arm when I went into the street.

I was a bit impatient with the Classics, even with Tolstoy and Balzac, and I remember, just after the War, I threw down to the floor a volume of Tolstoy – if even he, the great pacifist, couldn't prevent the slaughter of 1914-1918 and later the 1920s' Polish-Russian war. What good is even Tolstoy, if he couldn't prevent this murder, these blood baths? I couldn't read any book that was published before 1914. And, for a number of years, I read nothing but the latest books and poetry.

Every day we discovered new revolutionary geniuses in futurism, formalism, dada, and early expressionism. We couldn't make up our minds whether Picasso and Chagal, are revolutionary painters or if they are the product of Kapitalist Society? We have heard, and some even read, of the latest manifestos of the Surrealists as being before futurism. We have seen the moustache painted on Leonardo's Mona

Lisa. We have heard the cry to tear down all museums and picture galleries of yesterday. We applauded Mayakovksy and Yesenin, Tuwim and Breton.

I had discovered sex not so long ago, with a book which excited me terribly, and I read it with a greater passion and inner involvement than any other book. It was by the then most famous (and one of the first) Swiss sexologists, Auguste Forel, whose thick volume, *The Sexual Problem*, was read clandestinely by every adult young man and, rarely, by girls.

It was a revolutionary book. Freud was getting whispered about, but he too was read only by the most daring. I had stopped reading the Bible, and never opened a volume of the Talmud or any other Rabbinical book. It seemed so naïve, so remote, from the twentieth century which I had just discovered I was living in. Other revolutionary books which left a deep impression on me were a book, the very title of which was enough to frighten the life out of a religious man, it was by a German scientist called Ernst Haeckel called "*Moses or Darwin?*" The other book which I loved, and tried to model myself on, was *Rousseau's Confessions*.

I also, at this time, fell in love with a young girl of about fourteen years old (probably only because I read somewhere that Dante also fell in love with an even younger girl when he saw her for the first time), and I had on my table a coloured reproduction of a pre-Raphaelite painting of the poet meeting his Beatrice with her companion on a bridge. I couldn't make up my mind which of the three girls in Florentine dresses was his chosen one. All three looked conventionally pretty.

My colleagues used to chide me because I, a growing young man of eighteen, was in love with a fourteen year old girl. They too used to come to her father's house to play chess, and talk about literature, politics and philosophy. But above all to play chess, and drink the wine coloured Russian tea. The father was a good chess player and he nearly always won, even if he gave me a figure to start, but sometimes I used to beat him, which made me very pleased with myself.

Hersh Rosenblum was a socialist from his youth, and was a member of the Jewish Socialist Bund. His claim to fame was that he had been a prisoner in Siberia. The reader must remember that to have been sent as an exile to Siberia for a few years was a badge of honour, for the flower of the Russian and Polish intelligentsia had served in exile and hard labour in prison in the frozen Siberia. They were a few in our town who had been sent there for political activities, and we looked upon them as the heroes of our time. We gazed at them with love, and listened eagerly to their many grisly and harrowing tales.

Although more than twenty years had passed since Hersh Rosenblum had been exiled to Siberia for five years, when he came back he found he had tuberculosis, and he was a frail and ailing man. He was a man of ironic wit and common sense, and we would never tire of hearing from him stories of the Revolutionary movement and it's leaders, who were our heroes. We read their memoirs or biographies like the most exciting adventure stories. We knew the inside of a Siberian hut in the winter as well as we knew the Butyrka Shlissolburg and Petro-Pavlosk prisons.

From Rosenblum we heard all the fantastic stories about the Revolutionary Societies, *Ziemla y Wola*, Earth and *Narodowoltsy* (*Narodnaya Wolya*), the Peoples' Will; about the anarchists and the Social Revolutionaries, a leader of whom was to become, many years later, my friend in London.

With the exception of one book by Jules Verne, I did not read adventure stories, but the memoirs of Russian Revolutionaries and the names of Vera Zasulitch, Vera Figna, and Koropotkin, or reminiscences about Zhelabov and Sofya Perowskaya, were to me more interesting than the "Count of Monecristo" or the "Mysteries of Paris", or the stories of Sherlock Holmes.

Rosenblum's nineteen-year-old son, Meir, and his daughter Rosa, who was two years older, joined the Communist Party in spite of the fact that their father chided them, why they must join a party that insists on forming a government of "Soldiers and Peasants" – (the slogan of the Bolsheviks). I, who had the greatest admiration for the Russian Revolution, never attempted to join the Polish Communist party, mainly because I didn't like the way Stalin treated Trotsky who was, to us, a legendary figure. And even more so for the early killings in Russia of the Stalinist opposition, and the criminal intrigues they carried out against Socialists in Russia and in Western Europe. But Meir would argue that Stalin is the greatest revolutionary after Marx and Lenin, and he would assure me that within less than five years, the World Revolution will begin, and will abolish all iniquities and the exploitation of man will disappear. If only Trotsky, Zinoviev, Kamenev and Bucharin hadn't sold out to International Capitalism, and with sabotage, and the help of British, Japanese and German Imperialism, the Soviet Union would already be the greatest Socialist Fatherland of the Workers of the World.

If somebody would say something about the hunger and misery in Russia after the second five year plan, he would answer with the stock phrase that: "before you say the word "Soviet Russia" … you must first wash out your mouth!" Meir had learned the art of photography, and he went to stay in a neighbouring little town Brzeziny, where his parents came from and where they still had some relations.

One day he invited me to Brzeziny to stay with him. There, in the photographic studio of a mutual friend Alex Daum, he introduced me to a girl: Tall, buxom, with fine legs and shapely breasts, and with a face so beautiful that I thought I have never seen a more striking face in my life. She looked like the typical Jewish beauties out of the Bible; Sarah, Rachel, Rebecca, Ruth, romanticised Jewish figures which, in Poland and Russia distinguished themselves from the Slav women with their flaxen and golden hair … even if they were beautiful, Jewish beauty was altogether something oriental, something different, and they looked particularly exotic besides the flaxen and honey-coloured Slav women. There were two Jewish popular painters, Hirschenberg and E. M. Lilien, who liked to paint such Jewish beauties.

Her name was Bala, and it was love at first sight! Her father, I was told, is a rich Chassid and business man, who would never allow her to go out with an unbeliever, an apikores, and a Socialist, who, in the Summer now walks in the street without a hat, and eats Treyfus, non-Kosher food, and smokes on the Sabbath.

Bala had a lovely, dimpled smile. Her eyes, black and melancholy, looked shy, as if they had a secret to hide. She had two very thick locks falling round her oval face with its delicate skin. She smiled a lot out of shyness and showed a magnificent row of white teeth.

She was embarrassed, and when somebody in the studio introduced me as a budding writer, she asked me promptly if I knew a German writer, Franz Kafka. She said he was supposed to be one of the greatest writers who ever lived. He was going to marry her cousin; Dora Dumant, who had arrived yesterday from Berlin, and "You can meet her, if you like. She knows all about him. She'll come up in the afternoon."

"Franz Kafka?" I asked. "No, I never heard of him." And to myself I said, with the insolence of youth, what sort of great writer could he be if I have never heard of him. Not even the name have I seen before. What kind of provincial ignorance is this to make Franz Kafka "one of the most important writers of contemporary Europe!" And I had never even heard of him. Even if I haven't, what kind of writer could he be anyway?

"Dora, my cousin, will tell you all about him, and she will give you something of his to read," Bala said. We arranged to meet by the river in the evening at eight o'clock.

Her cousin, Dora, who had arrived in town only a day or two before from Berlin, was small, pale, narrow-chested, with small brown deep-set eyes, and thin legs in black stockings. She wore a black silken blouse and skirt. Her lips were dry and pale, and she had hardly any make-up on. Her dark brown hair, slightly fuzzy, was divided in the middle of her roundish head. She was one of those young women with a pale, sickly skin, whom one usually associates with a perpetual maidenhead – or who might be a member of a revolutionary party.

Dora smiled with her dry lips and dry teeth, and asked me if its true that I "write". "What sort of things do you write? Poetry, stories?" I stammered something about trying to write "little things".

"Kafka also wrote little things," she repeated. I admitted to her that I had never read anything of his, and for the first time I felt ashamed.

"You need not apologise," she said. "Nobody, except a few people in Germany and Czechoslovakia has ever heard of him, but all the writers in Prague, and particularly his friends, Max Brod and Franz Wefel, never published any of their works before showing them to Kafka for his opinion. And both of these writers thought of Kafka that he is a genius and a unique man.

I somehow knew the names of Max Brod and Werfel; whether I had actually read anything of theirs I don't remember, but their names were familiar.

"It's over a year since he died, and Max Brod is writing a book about him", Dora said. "I was with him for the last years of his life!" Her eyes were full of tears, but she controlled herself and didn't cry, but her face was grey, and a little spot of make-up began to melt around her left eye. She tried to condole me and said, "Of course you couldn't have read him, but I will give you two of his books which were published while he was alive, *Die Verwandlung* and *Der Hungerkünstler*." She took it for granted that I could read German, but she spoke to me in a fine Yiddish, full of Hebrew expressions, as good Yiddish usually is. Her Yiddish, spoken with a slight regional, almost folksy or folklorish accent from the province of Bedzin, near the East German frontier, had it's peculiar charm, and I was delighted with her strange expressions. She spoke about Kafka as if he were still alive. But it was Bala who told me about how Dora and Kafka were going to get married. She told me this before I actually met Dora. Kafka had written a letter to her uncle (Dora's father) and implored him for his consent to marry his daughter. Bala told me that Dora's father had shown the letter to the *Gerer Rebbe*, the Rabbi of Ger, a small town, called in Polish Gora Kalwezja, the most important Chassidic Seat, to which her own father used to travel. It was the most fanatical of all Chassidic Houses, which had the most zealous and the most powerful following in Poland, (I had myself, inherited a Chassidic dynasty from my father, The Skierniewice Chassidim, followers of the son of the Holy Rabbi of Worki – where my father was born).

The Gerer Rabbi said no to Franz Kafka's imploring letter, although he promised to be a good Jew. The refusal broke her heart because Dora was convinced that had her stern father consented to the marriage, Kafka might have lived. But, devoted, pious daughter that she was, she couldn't go against her father's will. And Kafka died not only of collapsed lungs but also of a broken heart. There was nothing in the world that he wanted more than to marry and to have a child with Dora. She was his last and greatest love. They couldn't marry because Dora's fanatical father, Bala's uncle, was against it. That last year when Dora was with him was the happiest year of his life. She had nursed him and looked after him for a year.

Dora came in again to the studio in the afternoon, and Daum, the owner, made us lemon tea in glasses. Dora, in her black dress with a black handbag in her hand, sat down in an old fashioned chair in front of the backdrop, which was painted to represent a palatial library in a gothic room. This served the photographer as a decoration for family portraits and groups. There were also other backgrounds; a garden in bloom, with apple trees and roses; a landscape with a little forest and a brook on the left and a path leading to hills in the distance. Bala and I were seated on a small settee by the window.

Dora told us how she left her father's Chassidic home, and went to Berlin just after the War. Once, when she was working in a home for Jewish orphan children, the Director announced one day that they may expect distinguished writers from Prague to visit the orphanage. She heard the names, Max Brod and Dr. Franz Kafka, for the first time. She knew nothing about them except that Max Brod was already a well-known writer and critic.

The first time that Kafka set eyes on Dora was in the kitchen which these writers were inspecting on their visit. She was preparing fish for the children's dinner, and her hands were dirty. Kafka passed by, smiling at her and she only heard him say: "Such beautiful hands, and already so bloody!"

She showed us a photograph of Kafka. He had deep, big burning black eyes, with heavy black eyebrows, and a hairline so low, that it hardly showed any forehead. He had a white shirt on with an elegant tie and a well-cut black suit. He had particularly big ears that stood out from his head. The most extraordinary thing was that, looking at the photograph, I thought that I knew someone who looked exactly like Kafka. He was a young man called Zachariasz, who was a younger brother of a Jewish socialist worker, and who had just recently tried to commit suicide by taking poison. Happily, he didn't die and was saved by his brother who called for help.

Later, when I accompanied Dora home, through the little winding streets, she told me many fascinating stories about Kafka: how, when he was ill, he told her stories with his hand and expressions on his face (he was not allowed to talk, only whisper). And he "talked" so expressively with his eyes and face muscles, that she could understand him perfectly. She also told me that his papers are being edited by his friend, Max Brod, who refused to obey Kafka's Will and Testament that all his works and writings (except the three little books already published in Berlin) should be destroyed.

When we parted near the prayer house, she told me that it would be better if I left her there, and not to go with her to the uncle's house, just like Bala, who wouldn't let me accompany her home either: "Uncle is very strict, a 'Burned' Gerer Chassid, like my father, and, like him he wont let his daughter go out with an Apikores (a free-thinker)!" I felt not a little flattered – having my fate linked with the fate of Franz Kafka.

Dora presented me with two books, *Die Verwandlung* (Metamorphosis) and *Der Hungerkünstler* (The Hunger Artist). I kissed her hand with gratitude and reverence, and went home. I was staying with Daum, the photographer.

That night, with a candle by my beside, I read *Die Verwandlung*. It read it through to the early hours of the morning. It made an extraordinary deep and frightening impression on me, like no other book ever had (except perhaps *Hamlet*, my own "discovery" with which I identified, or Dostoyevsky who, as the reader may remember from an earlier passage, had "almost the same ideas as I had about Christ and the Grand Inquisitor").

Next day when I met Dora at Daum's in the afternoon, she told me; "Now that you have read *Die Verwandlung* you should know that this Gregor Samsa, the man who wakes up one morning after terrible dreams, finds himself turned into a huge bug – a real *Ungeziefer*", is how Kafka himself felt in his father's home."

Dora told me that there are still a lot of manuscripts, stories, fragments, two completed novels, and a large diary, on which Brod is now working, even though Kafka had insisted that they be destroyed. The three little books he had published were all that he wished to remain of his works. Dora told me a nice little story: She said that after the *Verwandlung* had been published for three months, Kafka went into a big book shop and asked the salesman how many copies of his book had been sold. The man looked up his ledger, and said that already eleven copies had been sold. "Eleven copies?" Kafka repeated wonderingly. The salesman consoled him saying: "What do you expect, Dr. Kafka? Eleven copies of a new book by an unknown writer in three months, is good!" "No," said Kafka, "I am not complaining. You see, I only wonder who could have bought the other copy, because I bought ten copies myself."

I asked Dora what sort of books Kafka liked to read. She told me that he used to read a lot of Goethe, Kleist, Heine; a lot of Kierkergaard, Flaubert, Dostoyevsky, Balzac and Dickens and, of all people, Strindberg and other Scandinavians. His Prague contemporary friends, Brod and Werfel, would not publish anything without having it first read by Kafka. Dora told me that she taught him Hebrew and Yiddish. He was particularly fond of Yiddish, had a wide knowledge of both these languages, and she spoke Yiddish at home and read widely, in Yiddish and Hebrew, modern literature.

She was about twenty years old when she met Kafka, a shy and withdrawn girl. She had never heard his name until she heard from the Brod and Werfel circle that he was one of the greatest writers of all time.

Max Brod, in an article in the *Literasche Welte*, a weekly Berlin magazine, around which the new German writers grouped themselves, had said something unheard of before, that Kafka is of the importance to Goethe, and compared him with the greatest masters of European literature. His genius was dark but quite original.

CHAPTER FIFTEEN

I must here add that I am writing this with hind-knowledge of a vast literature about Kafka which started appearing long after Max Brod published his articles and his book on Kafka – the biography – as well as the novel on Kafka. The Kafka industry started just after the second World War, first in America, France, England and Germany. A lot of nonsense has been written about Kafka but, as a recent critic, Ernest Fischer I think, remarked: "Kafkaism will disappear, but Kafka will remain for ever."

At the time I am writing about of course I had no idea of Kafka's originality and profundity. First, I had not read his "*Castle*", his "*Trial*", or – the lesser – "*America*", neither his Diaries, all of which were published by Brod years after the death of Kafka, and I, with my Chassidic background, could not look into the heart of Kafka, which I tried to understand from the stories about him which Dora told me. I only knew that I had one great thing in common with him: Both he and I were rejected by two brothers who would not allow their daughters to marry freethinkers – Apikorsin, unbelievers.

This "almost" relationship with Kafka had a formative impression on me; I couldn't walk down the street with Bala, Dora's cousin with whom I had fallen in love. I saw her only once, sitting by the river, when she had put on a coloured peasant dress, and wrapped round her face a peasant shawl. We spoke of Dora and Kafka. She was afraid that Dora would do something desperate to herself. She looked ill, her skin was that greenish-grey that one felt afraid that she, too, might have consumption. But the most funny story was when Dora told me that Kafka wanted to open for himself and her a little restaurant, with Dora as the cook and Kafka as the waiter.

A few weeks later, Bala came secretly to town, and we told each other how much we loved one another, and we kissed ... but we did not make love. I thought that such things are not done with a virgin girl whom one *really* loved! Sex and love were kept apart. Sex, we felt, was a degradation of true love. I experienced this revulsion myself with a woman of about forty or forty-five, whose young daughter I thought I was in love with before I met Bala.

Her name was Lula and she was about thirteen. She was romantically pretty, with an oval, dark skinned face and brown, shiny eyes. I used to fondle her and kiss her passionately in corners, or whenever we went to the cinema, or for a walk in the evening in an unlighted street.

One day her mother asked me if and when I am going to marry her daughter.

"No!" I said, with some annoyance, because I didn't like the look of my future mother-in-law.

When she left my house she said she was running to the river, which divided half of the town, to thrown herself in! I felt she was just frightening me, and I didn't worry. What happened was rather as if out of a bad (or good) novel.

A few weeks before, when I was staying a night in her house, when her husband was in hospital, I fell a willing victim to this woman's contrived advances. In truth I cannot honestly blame her alone. I was as guilty as she was; I went to her bed that night – and I left her with a hatred of *all* women. I felt as if I had committed incest – and I could no longer look even at her young daughter. For the first time in my life I felt I had transgressed against the most fearful Jewish tabu. Here, I felt, was a kind of macabre story that Kafka could have written, perhaps even with bitter humour. But I couldn't write it. I tried to forget it.

And very soon afterwards I fell again into the clutches of sin.

A new batch of teachers arrived in our town for the Polish Gymnasium. One of them was a teacher of mathematics, Stefan Litwinski, who had a beautiful wife by the name of Jadwiga. She must have been about twenty-eight years old. She smiled at me with particular grace, as if she was genuinely pleased to see me, when I came up with an introduction from a colleague to her husband. They lived in a small flat with two rooms, a kitchen and a large sitting-double bedroom. There were books on shelves round the desk. On the wall facing it was a nude painting of a young woman, seen from the back, shoulder high down to the buttocks. It was of a well made woman, and the painting, in colour of living flesh was, it seemed to me, rather good. And from the delicate bone structure it was obvious that it was a portrait of the mistress of the house. I never asked if it was she. I was too shy – but I longed to see the picture from the front! I used to visit them quite often and borrow books.

One day we went for a walk into the woods, not far from the River Pilica, and the blue, bubbling source, called Molieskie Zrodla, where you could look to the bottom of the clear sky-blue water (it was famous in our district, and people from other towns and villages used to come to marvel at it, because looking down into the river, several metres deep, you could see the source and how the water bubbles up out of the sand).

It was near there in the pine wood that we used to sit in the clearing, sometimes taking with us a small basket of rolls and ham and cheese. Jadwiga (she must have been about thirty, and I only twenty), or Pani Jadwiga, as I used to call her respectfully, was always elegantly dressed, mostly in white or blue linen skirts with coloured blouses, and usually with a white and red ribbon round her brownish soft hair, which she wore short and parted in the middle.

She had full rounded lips, as if she was going to kiss, and revealed her white regular teeth. She laughed a lot at the slightest provocation and it did you good to hear her laughter. She had a curious little nose, only slightly turned up – as Polish noses usually are. She reminded me of the singer in the *La Boheme* which I had seen in the Warsaw Opera House, but she was more robust.

I never had the courage to kiss her. When we returned in the afternoon, just as it started to rain, she asked me to wait in the kitchen. As she changed in to something fresh and dry, she told me that I may come in to her room and I found her wearing a white peignoir with fine lace over her underwear. She was sitting on a high chair by the mirror and arranging her hair with a new silken ribbon. Suddenly, as I was facing her, peignoir fell open, and I could see the upper part of her upstanding breasts and the naked flesh of her thighs above the light silk stockings. She stood up, still and curiously innocent, looking at me as if the revelation of her half-naked legs had happened by sheer accident.

I took her by the arm with a movement towards the bed, but with gestures towards the sofa, she brought me back from my passionate rapture and merely said, quietly in cold prose: "The bed creaks ..." and she stretched out on the sofa by the window with several silk cushions. She kissed me and I returned her kisses passionately, and we made love – the first time with a woman of quality and of a forbidden race. She was not ashamed to exhibit without false shame a voluptuousness which was quite new to me, and which struck me for the first time – that women also like it!

When, after half an hour or so, she got up, went into the kitchen to make coffee, bringing back the tray with a coffee-pot, little cups and a sugar bowl, she stretched out again on the sofa, and together we drank the good black coffee. But when I bowed down to kiss again her half exposed legs, she wriggled herself gently free, and with motherly concern she said: "No! Too much isn't good for you!" Evidently she wasn't worrying about my or her own carnal desires, but only my wellbeing.

I left her house and walked the streets with a secret sense of power and pride: I had made love with a beautiful woman! It echoed in my ears: You just made love to a fine woman ... . And *nobody* knows about it – none of the passers-by in the street – No one guessed! And it seemed to me that I have some illusions of a Don Juan – or Casanova – It seemed to me that I carry in my heart a deep secret, and that I am man enough and adult enough not to boast of my conquest to anybody.

But I must admit that, though morally I felt the stings of remorse of having made love to a married woman, I, at the same time, also felt freed from my feeling of disgust, which almost turned to misogyny, because of the terrible woman, the mother of the girl I truly loved, and for whom I had felt revulsion, as if I were really smitten with the awful sin of incest.

I had promised Jadwiga to visit her in the evening at about eight o'clock. I rang the bell and she opened the door, and on seeing me she exclaimed in a manner of great surprise: "Ah! Pan!" As if I was the last person in the world she expected. I immediately understood that her husband, Litwinski, had returned and was in the other room. I marvelled at the wonderful deception that women were capable of and, as if I were wholly innocent, I pretended that I came to borrow a book, and left immediately. My heart was beating quickly and my conscience was itching me terribly.

I still lived with my aunt and uncle, and kept myself busy with dreams of the future, studying and reading all the time. History, philosophy, literature and religion – or rather anti-religion. Amongst them most I loved Heine, but I was overawed by the mighty genius of Goethe, and I adored Schiller and Lessing.

After having given up my earliest dreams of being the Messiah, or at least the assistant Messiah, I decided, as I have said, to become a writer, a poet, and finally a doctor or a psychiatrist. I wanted to understand the human mind and why it sometimes becomes sick. A book fell into my hands which gave me cause to worry. It was by that Italian, Jewish, psychiatrist, Cesare Lombroso (I loved his euphemous name), now only remembered by historians and a few students of criminology and psychiatry. The book was called, in German, *Genie und Irrsinn* (Genius and Madness). I read the book avidly, although I didn't understand some technical terms. As I was almost convinced that I am a genius, I nevertheless was suspicious about my sanity. The relationship of genius and insanity was, to me, as to Lombroso, quite obvious, and I was prepared to go a little mad for the sake of genius. Nietzsche was at that time my God, and I was afraid that my end will be like this. However I was convinced that I still have a long way to go. I remembered, as I said, that only a few years ago I asked myself the same question that Nietzsche asked in his autobiographical *Ecce Homo*: Why am I so clever? And the passages of *Zarathustra* that I had stolen and interpolated in letters to a girl in Lodz, who I thought I was madly in love with, must have made her think that I was already mad or going crazy!

Ever since those days I have been wondering why I have not gone mad, considering the many spiritual crises I have gone through in all the past years. We shall have to say something about this later on. Meanwhile, I was roaming around the world literature and was pleased to discover that Goethe invented the term, Welt-Literatur. Of course I knew Yiddish literature from Mendele to our contemporary Sholem Asch, who had already by then a world-wide reputation, and was translated into many languages. We read the great Russians, but above all I loved Chekhov. And I also decided to become a writer – but what kind of writer I didn't know. The verse I tried to write seemed to me jejune, even bad. A school friend, the grandson of my Rabbi, went with his mother to America to live together with his father. Within a year or two he became the editor of some Yiddish literary periodical whose name I forget. He asked me to send him some verse, which I did. It was, as I said, pretty bad, but he corrected it and cut it, and printed it in his magazine. When he sent me a copy I thought that my poetry was even worse than when I wrote it. I continued writing for the local papers.

My uncle and aunt lived in my house with me. She would do the cooking, sometimes making special delicacies for me. With her husband she quarrelled constantly, and at least once a week they went to the local town Rabbi to get a divorce.

I hated living with them, and used to lock myself in my room with my books.

I had no money except for the little hand-outs she used to give me to buy some luxuries, such as grapes and oranges. She was a good but messy woman, and went around in her old long, soiled dresses reaching to her ankles. I am afraid I was sometimes unkind to her when she used to annoy me and kept on asking me when I am going to find a nice bride. She was looking around for a nice, rich Jewish girl. I was sixteen when my mother died, so it was my aunt who tried to take her place and marry me off to the right girl. She once described one to me; how beautiful she was, by gesturing over her breasts with her hands extended over her neck: "Such a beauty!" Meaning how fat she is.

I was often cruel to her when she lavished her love and praise on me as if I were her own son. She would stuff me with soups, meat and compotes, and cake which she cooked herself, and her matzos balls were really delicious. I was too thin; I was too pale; and the remedy was to eat and to drink innumerable cups of sweet tea with lemon, or milk and honey, or a soft boiled egg in chicken soup. She, herself, was stuffing herself all day long, and she would eat two or three pieces of cake dipped in a syrupy wine.

In the morning she would bring me into my room twenty rolls, butter, and a bowl of sour cream.

As I was sure that, as a writer, I shall have to starve later on (as I read in most biographies of famous poets and writers that they did), I prepared myself for this future hunger and ate huge breakfasts, dipping the rolls in the cream. On one particular occasion I remember polishing off eighteen rolls with butter and a glass of coffee in order to withstand the hunger which surely awaited me in later years.

In reading the biographies of famous writers, I saw that for every poet or writer born rich, like Tolstoy and Turgenev or Byron and Shelley and Goethe, hundreds of celebrated writers were born poor, and some lived in poverty for the rest of their lives.

So I surmised that the more I shall eat now, the more I shall stuff myself with good things – the more strength will I have to survive later when I shall be forced to go hungry – as I was certain will happen to me.

I was a poor young rich man. I say "rich" by the standards of our town, but I really had no money except for the rent from two or three families who lived on the upper floors of my house, with the exception of a tailor's widow who didn't pay because she had nothing to pay with, and she hired herself out as a daily woman once or twice a week.

Then, just before I was twenty-one years old, my uncle had the cunning idea of advancing me money every month, and for which he demanded from me a written I.O.U. that I had received so much from him. He gave it to me in driblets of a few hundred zlotys a month. I couldn't sell the house before I was twenty-one.

Meanwhile I lived like a rich young man of private means, But within a year my uncle informed me that he had paid me for half the property, and I had to go with him to a solicitor and sign over to him half of the house.

I bought books and more books – a whole library of them. I remember coming back once with a droshky load of big parcels of books. Travelling with me was Mr. Nirenberg, who thought of himself as an intellectual of the town, and knew me. "What have you got in all these parcels?" he asked me. When I said "books", he asked me whether I am going to open a lending library (there was only one in the town, and a free Jewish public library in the Socialist Club, and one in the Zionist Society).

"No," I said, "I just bought them for myself!"

"What? Are you going to open a book shop?"

"No!" I assured him. "I bought them just for myself to read." I had to tell him what the books were and he, amazed at my deep thirst for culture and great books, shook his head, baffled, incredulous and astonished.

I was soon the owner of a select private library, but I also had access to the magnificent library of Mr. Antoniewicz, a civilized and kind Pole, the Director of the college where he used to lecture on such subjects as the Bahagavad Gita, Gitangali, and other Sanskrit and Buddhist writings, which interested me greatly. I was fascinated by Yogi literature but, above all, I loved Buddha of all spiritual leaders, although I realized, as soon as my knowledge of the history of religion widened, that Buddhism is a long arduous way of peaceful dying, and that Judaism is a religion of joyful and compassionate living. (A love of life which Schopenhauer could never forgive Jewish optimism.)

I used to love Mr. Antoniewicz's lectures, and I liked his kindly wrinkled face with his full lips and white teeth, and when he smiled he showed two upper left side teeth missing.

In the afternoons he would invite me for a chat in his library. He talked to me about modern Polish literature, about Zeromski, Przybyszewski, and Telmaiez, and the young Polish poets who were leading the new literary movement, the Skamandriey (they were grouped around the monthly Review *Skamander*), with Julian Tuwim, Antoni Slonimski and Jan Lechon. But, above all, I was grateful to him for giving me the key to his library, where I could sit and read in comfort, or take home as many books as I liked. Another acquaintance I made was a rich young man who was known in the town as the *Prince of Wales* (Ksiaze Walji, in Polish) of Tomaszow, and in truth he was not only the most elegantly dressed man, wearing the latest English fashions, but was also the most handsome man, who resembled the most popular romantic actor of the day, Rudolph Valentino.

I had, by that time, through reading some famous novels and looking through French, German and Polish Art magazines and literary periodicals, decided to become a dandy (I liked the word) as some writers and poets whom I then admired, like Oscar Wilde whom I still believed to have been a maligned man as a homo-sexual (just as a few years ago, when I delivered my "revolutionary" lecture on Wilde, I refused to read anything about his inversion, because I just couldn't believe that such men exist when there are so many beautiful women in the world). I stood by my naïve, stupid theory, that British Imperialists and the reactionaries were bent on destroying him, and I even toyed with the idea of writing under Wilde's pseudonym of Sebastian Melmoth, when he went away to France, to die there in poverty in a third-class hotel.

Chapter Sixteen

The way I came to meet Henry Landsberg, whom we called Henio, was rather out of the ordinary. I had just been reading a second-rate novel by the American, Upton Sinclair (whom we admired for his Chicago book, "The Jungle") I forget its title but it told a story of a very rich man who makes friends with a poor, aspiring boy and then lets him down. It was a mediocre book, and I was dreaming of someone who would discover me. I thought that the best way would be if I were to meet a man like Henio, the heir of the richest manufacturer in Tomaszow, with whom I thought I had at least something in common. He, too, lost his father in a tragic way: He committed suicide by jumping out of a window from the fourth floor of a psychiatric hospital.

He was the richest man in town and left two big woollen factories, which were competing with the best English cloth, and dealers and tailors would say, fingering a piece of cloth: "It's the best – if it's a piece of Landsberg's Kamgarn (worsted)." He also left a magnificent house which the town called the Landsberg Palace. "It's a piece of Landsberg Merchandise." No higher praise was needed in Poland.

I had seen Henio Landsberg, the heir to that vast fortune, several times in the street in the summer, dressed in a white or blue jacket and cream coloured trousers, when he had just come back from a game of tennis, or in the latest foreign-cut elegant suit, usually without a hat and displaying a fine head of beautifully combed dark hair riding in a carriage with a liveried driver in front of him, and very often in an open sports-car of some foreign make – which must have been unique in town.

He really looked like the Prince of Wales, except that Henio had a little slightly curved dark moustache. He was tall, perhaps well over six foot, and very handsome with a fine figure and he walked lightly like a dancer.

I went into the side-streets, not far from my home where his "Palace" stood in a tree-lined garden. It looked to me like one of the French nineteenth castles that I knew from illustrations.

I made up my mind that I must try myself with the veracity of literature, and prove to myself that books do not always tell the whole truth. As I approached the Palace, which was surrounded by a tall spiky iron rail, I came to the huge black iron gate, shining at the top in a newly painted gold colour. Inside the gate by a small white and black hut sat the gate-keeper with a rifle in his hand and two enormous wolf-hounds at his side. He stopped me and asked in a polite voice whom I am going to see. "Pan Henryk Landsberg", I said. "He's away, I think. I haven't seen him today, but you can go and inquire inside."

I went up to the house and rang the bell by the side door, and looked through the glass doors at the long, elegantly furnished corridor with pictures on the wall.

A maid in a white bonnet came to open the door with an inquiring look on her broad shining peasant face. "Pan Henryk is away and wont be back until Monday evening. Who shall I say has called?" she asked me. I didn't give my name as I knew he wouldn't know it, but said that I'd call on Monday evening after dinner.

On the following Monday I called on Henryk Landsberg at his "palace", around eight o'clock. A uniformed woman let me in and showed me into a small reception-room full of paintings and elegant Empire furniture.

Along the corridor on both walls there were drawings by a painter, who seemed to me, of extraordinary power, in black and white which I had never seen before, or even heard of. It was Daumier, and I had never seen anything of his – and even the name was new to me. The first painter I had discovered for myself. (Later I discovered two other painters about whom I had never read a word: Cezanne and El Greco.)

Within minutes Henryk Landsberg came in to the room in a silken coloured dressing-gown. He invited me with a welcoming gesture to his study.

It was a large room with windows onto the garden, and was elegantly furnished in light colours. There were book-shelves with especially bound books in red and black morocco and some in coloured silk and linen. On the shelves were a few modern books on paintings – none of the painters did I know except one, who impressed himself on my mind: A Picasso of the early cubist period was on the wall and a portrait by Modigliani (which I was proud to recognise without looking at the signature). I had read something about Picasso and I had been discussing only a few days before, with an acquaintance of mine, the merits and de-merits of modern art. He was a communist and his theory was that Picasso was a symptom of Capitalist decay! That he was *not* a revolutionary painter.

There was one thing in the room which I didn't like and which puzzled me; in an elegant silver frame there was a photographic portrait of Benito Mussolini, and I was shocked to discover, as a good Socialist, that the rich seemed to be admiring the Fascist leader even in our small town, whom we despised, although we did not yet know of the wide-spread tyranny he was to cause.

Henryk showed me to an enormous fine easy-chair of dark blue velvet, which matched the colour of the velvet curtains at the windows. I gazed at the shelves of teak-wood, with rows and rows of de luxe editions of books, on the walls, and at the fine electric lamps on the side-tables and behind my chair, with lamp shades of some old illuminated manuscripts which I couldn't read.

Henryk asked me whether I drink coffee or tea, or perhaps some wine, sherry or port? I am afraid I felt more uneasy by the exquisite luxury by which I was surrounded, than by the fact that I didn't know the difference between sherry and port! Above all I felt a bit self-conscious about the shoes I was wearing, though they were polished, they were not new and slightly out of shape, and looked almost vulgar when standing on that magnificent Persian carpet, which dazzled me with its subdued colours like a fine master painting.

I felt it was almost sacrilege to stand on such a piece of oriental beauty in my common old shoes. And when I sat down I raised one foot from the other off the carpet. I was not ashamed of my new suit, although made by a small provincial tailor it fitted me quite well and was, moreover, of a material which Landsberg immediately recognized as of his own manufacture.

I was freshly shaven and had eau-de-cologne on my face and powder. My hair was combed with a quinine lotion. My tie was new and of fine quality, bought in the best shop in town, with a quiet pattern of blue and white tiny dots; I had on a freshly ironed shirt, beautifully white, which I had got out from the laundry only an hour before. Yet I felt provincial, dreary, tasteless and small-town elegant, (as I used to see in the illustration of popular novels) compared with the rich magnificent dress of Landsberg, who was now wearing a spectacularly beautiful silk dressing-gown of some delicate Chinese design. A white heavy silk shirt, open at the neck which, instead of a tie, had a dark green silk handkerchief round it, the sort of thing I had only seen worn by the stars of films.

But above all I was admiring the colours, the delicate design of the carpet, which covered the whole room and had a big white polar bearskin rug over it which was spread in front of the fireplace. I was scared that I might soil this magnificent carpet which, I gathered, must be Persian, with my shoes – although I took the trouble to clean them of the mud and had polished them with a fresh tin of best shoe-polish before leaving home.

Pan Landsberg was wearing a pair of fine, elegant dark blue suede slippers with his initials "H.L." embroidered on them in gold thread. He sat down opposite me on the long sofa. The maid had brought in on a silver tray coffee and pastries and had put them down on a mahogany antique table. He asked me whether I take milk or cream. I said, "Black, please!" in honour of the great coffee drinker Balzac, whose biography I was then reading.

Henio Landsberg questioned me pleasantly about my life, and asked me where I lived. Apparently he had heard something to the effect that I am one of the younger intelligentsia of the town, but that I came from a very religious Jewish family, from Chassidim, and that I wanted to become a "European", meaning a modern Western man, and that I don't practise my religion. I told him how I had witnessed my father's murder (he had heard about this but knew no details). He commiserated with me that I must have experienced a terrible shock. He spoke, in an aristocratic, nasal Polish with an affectation, whereas I spoke slowly, rehearsing mentally many a sentence inwardly, to get it grammatically right, though my accent was not too bad. He mentioned only in passing that he knew what losing a father means. I was not sure whose death was more tragic, his father's or mine; My father, at least, was a martyr, a small compensation which, I thought not without vanity, made me some kind of remote Jewish hero – a victim of anti-Semitism. His father, Alexander Landsberg, died because he was too rich, certainly the richest man in town, and by his own hand.

I told him that I had sold half my house which I had inherited, and that I am planning any day now to go to Warsaw, and if I can to go eventually abroad to Berlin, Paris and Vienna, the three cities where culture of Europe is being made. The extraordinary thing was that London didn't come into my fantasies. I knew absolutely nothing of England. Nobody in town knew anything either, and I had never met a man who could speak English. England was a remote country at the very end and on top of Europe. It was, of course, a mysterious land enveloped in constant thick fog and rain, but from that dark, unknown island, England was running (by some highly ingenuous intrigues and political power), the greatest Empire in the whole history of the world. It is the richest country in Europe, richer with her Empire than even America.

The truth was that England never bothered to make her culture known as the French did (who language was obligatory in our schools as a second language), and since the seventeenth and eighteenth centuries French was the language of the Polish and Russian aristocracy.

"But how will you live?" Landsberg asked me.

"I want to be a writer," I said.

"But it takes years for a writer, until he becomes known to make a living."

"Then I will go to Warsaw first and try to get work on a Yiddish newspaper."

"Yiddish? You mean Jargon?" *Jargon* was the word that the Yiddish language was called by the assimilated Jews who tried, by lessening their Jewishness, to parade their Polish patriotism.

Henryk Landsberg was a convinced assimilator, or a Pole of the Religion of Moses (Wyznania Mozeszowego) and, like assimilated Jews – particularly German Jews – he despised Yiddish which is the language of the ghetto and the common people.

We young Jews, who wanted to get away from Hebrew because it chained us down to the Talmud and Rabbinical literature, or even of the so called provincial literature of the Haskala (enlightenment) with their bourgeois and conservative criticism of Chassidism, whereas Yiddish was a young, vigorous and creative language over five hundred years old, that had, in the last half century, overtaken Hebrew with a powerful literature in prose and poetry. Whereas Hebrew has only one or two major poets (and even they wrote poetry in Yiddish too), hardly a single novel of importance had been written in that language.

Yiddish had just as humble a beginning as Anglo-Saxon which, with the development of the Elizabethans, became the richest and most widely spoken language in the whole world.

Yiddish is a much poorer language than English, but it adequately expressed the soul of the majority of the Jewish people in Eastern Europe, some seven or eight million souls in Poland, Russia, Lithuania, Latvia, Austria, whose National language was Yiddish. Yiddish was also a lingua franca to millions of Jews in U.S.A., South America and Australia. The masters of Yiddish had in the course of less than one century created a unique literature which started with Mendele Mochar Sforim, Sholem Aleichem, Peretz and Sholem Asch, our greatest contemporaries. Hebrew had one little four-page newspaper in Warsaw, the *Ha-Tsfira*, and Yiddish had four big daily papers, and several periodicals in Warsaw alone, not to mention the great and rich Press in New York, and a widely scattered press in the provincial towns, the smallest of which was "my own" Weekly newspaper, which was printed in Piotrków, a neighbouring town, where I had one page.

We had excellent black coffee and dainty pastries, which looked more like cut pieces of a chocolate and cream tart, and I couldn't make up my mind with what to eat it, with a knife, fork or spoon. I waited for Landsberg and he noticing my predicament, smiled, and took his pastry with his fingers which he later licked, and wiped his hand with a fine pink coloured linen napkin.

I told him that I wanted to leave Tomaszow and go to Warsaw, "There is no future for me here."

"Yes!" He said, "But how will you live?"

"I've still got a few thousand zlotys from the sale of half my house, and I will try to get on a Yiddish newspaper in Warsaw."

"I had an idea," said Landsberg, "Next week we are having Julian Tuwim to stay with us for a few days, and I will introduce you to him."

"That will be wonderful", I said, "I adore Tuwim immensely and I have read all his published books and poetry."

Tuwim was the most famous of the younger generation of Polish poets, and he was probably the greatest poet in the Polish language since Mickiewidz, a century before. Tuwim, Antoni Slonimski, Lechow, and Iwaszkiewicz, were the poets most widely read. They grouped themselves around the weekly literary magazine, *The Wiadomoici Literinckie*, and the monthly *Skamander*, two periodicals on the best European model which I used to read avidly and religiously. I also subscribed to the Yiddish weekly *Literarishe Bletter* and the German *Literarishe Welt*, the radical *Die Weltbuhne* and *Das Tagebuch* and *Simplizisimus*. In addition I was an avid newspaper reader; I read at least two or three newspapers a day; Warsaw papers of course and Berlin and Viennese papers, (provincial papers, including our own didn't count). I didn't buy all these papers, with the exception of the literary review I bought only one paper which was delivered after eleven o'clock, and the others I borrowed from the shop (paying only a few groszy for the loan) and which I returned later in perfect and uncrumpled condition, having read them through from cover to cover.

I was preparing myself for the journey to Europe to escape from the misery and hatred of Poland, and the great fear that was in every Jew's heart.

Meanwhile Landsberg invited me to come again on the following Saturday to dinner, when he would introduce me to Julian Tuwim and another important guest who might be helpful to me. I left the

Landsbergs that evening with a feeling that I had been invited by the Rothschilds!

The following Saturday evening I went again to the palace with a trembling heart and in great expectation of meeting and dining with the most famous poet of Poland.

Julian Tuwim, who had a slender figure and was elegantly dressed, had an unforgettable face; it was sharp and angular with a strong chin and a long nose like Dante's, grey-blue eyes, with a head of light coloured hair, and a most peculiar dark, large, purple birth-mark on the left side of his face – as if it were burnt skin. He had full curved lips, and when he smiled, as he often did, he showed two rows of strong, longish teeth, slightly yellowed like old ivory from constant smoking. He spoke in a most musical and fine Polish of the aristocracy with a University education, as if he were reciting a poem (which he often did) publicly.

He was the son of an impoverished Jewish book-keeper, and was born in Lodz, known as the second Manchester – just as our town was called the Third Manchester because of the highly developed manufacture of woollens and cottons and linens produced in Lodz which were exported to the whole of Russia and to other countries abroad.

At first sight the purple birth-mark on Tuwim's face looked like a splash from an ink bottle and made an unpleasant, and even frightening, impression, but when you got used to that scar which looked like a closed wound his face took on an uncanny look, and you thought of an original Dantesque face, which might have been stamped by the Evil One – by Satan – to distinguish him from other sinners. There was something Mephistophelian in his face, yet it seemed a mark of distinction of a highly original man, and when you came to know him you saw what a kind and good man he was.

We sat in two deep chairs in a corner of the big reception room, and talked of many things; of his translation of French and Russian poets, chiefly Baudelaire and the tragic Rimbaud, who gave up writing poetry at the age of twenty and became a gun-runner in Abyssinia, and had gangrene of the leg which had to be amputated, and which shortened his life and caused him great suffering.

We talked about Yesenin and Myakowsky, and even of Pushkin whom Tuwim had translated in a masterly version. (The names of Pushkin and Gogol were the very first writers I had ever heard of; Before I could even read a neighbour of ours, a girl whose brother was my school-mate, won a first prize on finishing at her gymnasium, and was presented with two volumes by Pushkin and Gogol, two names which sound to me both wonderfully comic!)

Gently Tuwim probed my knowledge of European literature and, I think, was satisfied by my non-ignorance.

"I hear you want to come to Warsaw," he said. "That's a very good idea; I'll introduce you to a few people. Incidentally, could you translate *War and Peace*? We are trying to get out a new translation."

"No," I said, "unfortunately my Russian isn't good enough for such a work."

We talked about a dozen other literary matters of both the old and the new. We found ourselves alone in the study when a butler announced in his grave voice that dinner is served.

We went into the large dining-room where Mrs. Landsberg, dressed in a violet dress with a single pearl necklace round her neck, one large diamond ring (with a black pearl, I thought). She was a tall, elegant woman in her early fifties, but one could still see the remains of a former beauty. She was a handsome woman with a strong magnificent graying hair.

I was relieved that no one was in evening dress (or, as it is called in Polish, "Smoking"), because I didn't have an evening suit and had never worn one. I had managed, however, to have my dark suit pressed. There was another guest standing by the table, a man with a short corpulent figure, elegantly dressed, with a handsome well shaven face, which made his cheeks look almost blue. I was told earlier that he was a rich banker from Warsaw known for his philanthropic work. His name, when I was introduced to him by Landsberg, was given as Silberman. Apparently Tuwim knew him too.

"What have you two been discussing?" Landsberg asked Tuwim as we entered.

"Oh!" said Tuwim. "The two wise men of Zion were discussing the secrets of World literature."

This was an ironic allusion to the notorious anti-Semitic hoax which was then translated into Polish, as it was into most European languages, and became the "Bible" of all anti-Semites – from the motor manufacturer Henry Ford to a man called Hitler (who, with Ford's money published it in Germany and in other countries, both in Europe and America). The book was called *The Protocols of the Wise Men of Zion*. This malevolent, false document was, at the time, exposed by the London *Times* as a forgery, so we read in our Jewish press, and that no Gentile of some literary culture believed a word of it. Yet it had a tremendous influence in Poland and was bought by semi-literate people who normally don't buy books of any kind. Besides it was quoted daily in the anti-Semitic press, particularly in the official anti-Jewish organ the *Kurjer Warsawski*, or *Twa Grosze* (as it was called, because it cost two pennies).

Pan Silberman sat at the table on the right hand side of Pani Landsberg and Tuwim on her left, I sat next to Tuwim and Landsberg at the other end of the table.

It was an excellent dinner with black caviar to start, then a delicate soup and then trout, after which came a meat dish of a peculiar flavour which I had never tasted before, but which tasted delicious and somewhat spicy and sweet. I had trouble enough choosing the right spoon or fork from the silver cutlery set before me, and I was watching Tuwim to see which knife and fork he picked up.

Mr. Silberman explained in a deep voice the intricacies of banking and the wider reasons for the economic crises, and he discussed Marshal Pilsudski and his government, and whether he is as much an anti-Semite as Roman Dmowski and Grabski.

Though the whole company at the table were (with the exception of myself) convinced "Poles of the Mosaic Faith", i.e. complete assimiliationists, and I the only Jewish Jew, the conversation was uneasy, and Silberman hinted that the crisis and the economic pressure on the Jewish businessmen and shopkeepers will not lessen, and the boycott will not stop, and people with a little money for the fare were trying to leave for Palestine and America, The Leaders of the anti-Semites were the Endeks, the National Democrats, who fulminated daily in their press against the Jewish-Masonic Bolshevik plot to enslave Poland.

Tuwim, sitting next to me, said something about his distinction of being attacked almost daily, together with Slonimski another poet and satirist.

The coffee with liqueurs were served in the small salon, with silken covers in gold on the big, comfortable chairs. We smoked Egyptian cigarettes and Silberman lit a huge Havana cigar. He asked me when I am coming to Warsaw, and if I do to come and see him. Pan Landsberg will give me the address. And Tuwim invited me to look him up as soon as I arrive in Warsaw.

Leaving before anybody else, as I gathered that Silberman and Tuwim were staying with the Landsbergs, I thanked them for the invitations and went home in a hopeful mood, and proud of myself that I had met the most famous poet, who had, I thought, a special sentiment for Tomaszow as his wife, an elegant light-haired charming woman, was a native of our town and a daughter of a local Jewish business man, Marchev, which I took as a good omen that our town is so closely connected with a celebrated poet whom, above all others writing in Polish and mentioning often our little town Tomaszow, and the river Pilica which cut our town in half.

CHAPTER SEVENTEEN

I went home alone through the badly lit streets to my dark, gloomy house, which I hated. I was afraid of my own shadow and was often in a panic on hearing the sound of my own footsteps. This horrible fear had never left me since that winter Friday evening when my father was shot in front of my eyes, and when my mother and I were, as if by a miracle, spared. This fear never left me whenever I went home alone late at night. Normally I would meet my colleague Moishe, who came practically every evening to the Rosenblums house where we talked, read the new books from the library, and argued about literature and politics, or played chess (a game which I usually lost to old Rosenblum but won from Moishe).

As the Rosenblums lived almost in poverty, we would buy the sausages and fresh ham in town and bring them to their home, where we had a communal Kolacja – evening meal (our dinners were usually at 3 o'clock p.m.). Mrs. Rosenblum made delicious tea with lemon, but the tea was so aromatic that I drunk it with sugar only and without lemon, which changed the colour of the tea and made it look pale and lose its specific Russian wine colour of the tea as well as the tangy aromatic flavour.

Meir, the son, worked in the same photographic studio as my latest love, the unfortunate Bala – the cousin of Dora Dimant the last woman in Kafka's life, whose fanatical father was against the marriage, as Bala's father was afraid of my marriage to his beautiful daughter. He would, he declared, rather die than that his daughter should marry an unbeliever, Godless and a Socialist Apikores (Epicurean). Of all Greek philosophers not the Stoics nor the Cynics, nor the Sophists, were so feared as the Epicureans. The Talmud and the Medroshim are full of warnings against him.

"Da ma she'Toshev l'Apikores" – Know what to answer an epicurean – is repeated by the Rabbis, during the Hellenist Period, many a time. Because, of all the Greek philosophers, the most hated were the followers of Epicurus. They not only denied the existence of gods, but their goal was the enjoyment of pleasure in this world and not in the World to Come.

Meier and their daughter, Ruzka, were fanatical communists, and if you dared to say a word against Stalin you were a traitor and an enemy of the working classes. They both went to conspiratorial cell meetings, discussed the World Revolution, which was expected to join the Russian Revolution and free Mankind, and above all the toiling and exploited masses would be loosened from the chains of Capitalism. They also risked imprisonment, distributing propaganda leaflets and clandestine communist newspapers and magazines.

As I used to be seen walking the streets with some of the agitators, the Police kept an eye on me and my mail, particularly the books that I used to get from abroad, were tampered with.

One night, it was after twelve o'clock and I was reading in bed and preparing to go to sleep, when there was a violent knocking at my front door.

The Police! A harsh common voice shouted: "Open up!" I unlocked the door and two policemen, armed with rifles and revolvers, and a man in civilian clothes entered through the kitchen and into my room. They looked into every book and magazine and threw them on the floor. They opened the drawers of my writing-table and looked into the cupboards in search of illegal literature. They went through my correspondence and picked up a bundle of expensive pink envelopes with a black ribbon round them. The man in civilian clothes put the bundle in a leather bag. I told him – "This is my private correspondence from a girl I love, and I don't want you to read them!"

He furiously tore open one letter (although he could more easily have taken it out without tearing the envelope) "We shall see about that! You are not here to tell us what to do," he said in anger.

"Prosze Pana, please sir!" I pleaded naively with him, "Just smell these letters and you'll see that they are perfumed with expensive scent!" They can't be political letters!"

"I decide such things," he said in fury, and began looking through every book on the shelves and the table and found some manuscript copy books and loose sheets of writing. He also found on the walls three portraits of dangerous looking revolutionaries, of Darwin, Marx and Tolstoy, which he confiscated. They looked suspicious to him because of their long white beards.

I was arrested and taken under guard to the police-station in an old car. I felt almost ashamed of *not* being a Communist, because the men who made the search and confiscated my love letters represented to me capitalist "law and order".

I sat in a dark, small cell all night and fell asleep on the bunk only when the early morning gray-blue of the sky broke through the barred top window. At about ten o'clock a policeman in uniform opened the door and asked me to accompany him to the chief of the police. Earlier, at about eight o'clock, I had been given a huge tin mug of tasteless tea and a chunk of dry black bread. A drank the watery tea – I didn't touch the bread – and I was hungry.

In the corridor I saw some prisoners and young Meier Rosenblum among them. I was not allowed to talk to him, and he turned to me with his back, pretending not to know me. The chief of police, a man of enormous size, with a cruel face and a huge yellowish moustache, whom I used to see riding in a droshka several times in the streets of our town, unexpectedly smiled at me – or rather – contorted his fat lips to resemble an imitation of a smile.

My bundle of letters were in front of him, all almost opened with the envelopes torn.

"So you are a Communist in love?" He said with heavy irony.

"No!" I answered, "I am in love, but I am not a Communist party member; I am a Socialist!"

"To me you are all the same," he said.

"The Polish Socialist Party (P.P.S.) is legal and represented in the Sejm (Parliament). The Jewish Socialist party, the Bund, is legal and has its members on the Warsaw County Council," I retorted.

"Don't tell me about legality. I know all about that. But I see that you know some important people. Dr. Narewski telephoned me and said that he guarantees for you that you are a law-abiding citizen. I shall let you go this time, but remember, if you are not careful and keep company with these agitators, I'll keep you here under lock and key."

What had happened was that my aunt had gone early in the morning to Dr. Narewski and begged him to intervene, as nobody knows how innocent of political agitation I am better than he.

He handed me over the bundle of letters. "The pictures I'll keep. Now let me not see you here again," he said.

Meier, I learned later, was arrested the same night with some twenty other men and young women. His sister, Ruzka, told me that he was denounced by a provocateur, and that a parcel of illegal leaflets and other Communist literature were found by the police in his rooms. Her fiancé, a young, good-looking man from Lodz, and the organizer of the region, was arrested a few days earlier.

A month or so later, I was told, Meier and the twenty other suspects were sentenced to from two to three years imprisonment. Meier was one of those who got three years in the provincial capital Piotrków, not very far from our town. A group of sympathisers of the revolutionary movement were collecting money from workers in the factories for a rescue action for the prisoners. I contributed a little myself and gave it to Ruzka. The idea was, I was told in great secrecy, to help him and three others to escape from prison with the help of "*delid*" – a "greased" (bribed) prison guard, and to get him false papers to cross the frontier to Russia from a village near Wilno.

When we had the first greetings from the Socialist father-land, Russia, we celebrated with a huge bottle of Vodka and smoked herring.

Ruzka passed her matric at the Gymnasium and went to the university of Warsaw studying Germanistics.

I prepared myself for the journey to Warsaw with prospects of recommendations from Tuwim and the banker, Silberman. A year before, I had been to Warsaw and, having a vague idea that I wanted to study medicine, I was taken by a colleague of the Faculty, the student Glass, to the operating theatre in the main building on Krakowskie

Przedmiescie. I witnessed the operation on an old woman of about 55 or 60 years. I regret to say that my visit was not a success; though I was dressed in a white coat, a white cap and could observe every movement of the operation, (it was, I think, a cancer in the eye) I didn't feel too well watching it, and within minutes I was prostrate on the floor and had to be lifted up by two students and carried out of the operating theatre into the corridor. And that was the end of my medical career.

Shortly afterwards I packed my case and left again for Warsaw. This time I took with me a four volume de luxe edition of Heine in the original, which I had hoped to sell to a second-hand bookseller, which I did the very next morning after having spent a pleasurable night in a Turkish bath, and treated myself to sandwiches and beer after midnight and after the refreshing baths – both Roman and Turkish, and a Vichy Douche. Considering that I spent the rest of the night after the bath in a comfortable, clean bed in a separate room, which served me as a hotel, it was not expensive at all.

I sold the Heine with a sorrowful heart and regret, because Heine was, at that time, one of my favourite poets. But, I thought, as soon as I make some money I could always buy them back. Then I went straight to 26, Krolewska Street, just at the corner of the large main street, Piotrkowska and opposite the Ogrod Saski (the Saski Gardens) Warsaw's nicest park in the centre of the town.

Over the four-story building with wide windows, and on the ground floor windows, there were letters in gold proclaiming the firm's long-winded name: *BANK HANDLOWO W LODZI ODZIAL WARZAWSKI*, meaning simply: The Commercial and Industrial Bank in Lodz – Warsaw Branch.

I went in through the side door and, a little out of breath (which I tried to hide from the uniformed commissioner), I asked if I may see the President Pan Silberman. He asked me to sit down in one of the leather chairs that stood in a circle round a table with newspapers and magazines. When I gave the commissioner my name I noticed that he had a suspicious look on his pale face, as if he didn't get the impression that I am the kind of customer normally seen by the President, so I added to my name the name of my town and said that Mr. Silberman had asked me to call on him whenever I was in Warsaw when I had met him at my friends the Landsbergs.

He rehearsed before me the long message to show me that he understood what I said, and left me.

I sat and watched the row of clerks, with their big and long books before them and with bundles of bills of exchange, and other papers in front of them, as they sat behind a long counter and desks, which had printed notices displayed signifying their departments – Foreign Exchange – New Accounts etc. At the end of the hall was a cubicle with iron bars at the window where it said *Kassa* (Cashier) in big letters. Behind the bars I could see the bald head and shrunken grey, long, thin face – the cashier, presumably.

I waited no longer than five or ten minutes when the commissioner came back and announced to me (in a pleasanter voice than before!) that the Pan President will see me right away. Would I please follow him … and he guided me to his office at the end of the counters.

The office was business-like with an elegant desk with a stack of correspondence waiting for his signature. In a silver frame was a picture of two women, one young and the other older, and standing next to it a silver vase with two red roses.

Two big leather chairs were in front of the desk and Pan Silberman sat behind the desk in a comfortable swivel chair.

I felt very small in the low leather chair, and I was afraid that I might blush. I had by now met and spoken to many important people, but never to a banker.

Pan Silberman's imposing smile on his well shaven face, reassured me – as if he had decided to grant me a loan without collateral.

"So! You want to work and study in Warsaw?" He said, "There is no future for you in Tomaszow? From what Pan Tuwim and Pan Landsberg tell me you seem to be a bright young man with a promising career. But tell me first, have you found rooms? Where are you staying?"

I told him that I had arrived only yesterday and had stayed in a little hotel on the Agradowa. Silberman smiled and said that it is probably not as good as the Bristol (Warsaw's best hotel!), but that he would give me a letter to the director of the Jewish Students House, and hoped that he would find me somewhere there.

He picked up the telephone and spoke to somebody in another office, and asked him if he has a free moment to see a young man from Tomaszow and that something might be found in his department for him. He told him that I was with him now. "Yes," Silberman told me, "Director Szapiro will see you now, in about ten minutes." He called in his secretary and dictated to her a short note to the director of the New Jewish Students Home.

I went from Mr. Silberman's office to the other office behind a glass wall of the Bank director, Szapiro.

I knocked … hear a loud "proszce" (please), and went in. Director Szapiro didn't get up for me but remained seated behind his enormous desk. He was busy reading a paper and I could only see his enormous, hairless, white head with a full bulging face like a friendly dog.

"Oh yes! Come in. Sit down Mr. … Mr …"

I helped him out with my name. He finally put down the paper, made some pencil notes, and began – very slowly: "I hear from the President that you want to work with us here. Now tell me something about yourself; How old are you?" I told him I am twenty-four. He asked me whether I am good at figures, and whether I know anything about book-keeping and banking.

He asked me a few other questions … which I was afraid to answer truthfully.

"Well, when would you like to start? Next week? Shall we say Tuesday? Tuesday is the first of the month. I shall put you first in the Promissory Bills Department. I think you'll get on well with the head of the department. So I'll say good-bye now. I hope you'll excuse me. I have a lot of work to do … I just returned from Vienna."

I left Mr. Szapiro's office and crossed the street and went into Marszalkowska. I felt elated and grateful to Henry Landsberg who had introduced me to Silberman and Tuwim. Now, I was sure of a job, and that I shall not be starving in Warsaw and shall be able to devote myself to literature and philosophy.

I had been in Warsaw before; the first time father had taken me when I was about nine years old, but all I could remember was an enormous city with wide streets and big buildings, with thousands of people walking or waiting and crowding into big greenish-yellow trams.

The purpose of that visit was not to see Warsaw, but to be taken by my father to the old vast cemetery where the great Worki Rabbi, the grandfather of our present Rabbi of Skierice, one of the earliest disciples of the Baal Shem, the founder of Chassidism, was buried.

We went by cab and horse through the teeming Jewish quarters, the Nalewki, where I was struck by the Jewish signs in Hebrew lettering on most of the shops; Where Jews from the provinces (and Christians) came to buy wholesale from the Jewish businesses. I was frightened by the huge cemetery, which I couldn't see properly, for it's plain grave stones and marble slabs – like the proverbial "woods for it's trees". Here and there there was a little house, four-walled with an open door, not bigger than a peasants' forest cottage. These were the graves and sarcophagus of the Holy Tzadik, which were surrounded by a wooden partition, a perpetual oil lamp – a *ner tonid*, and some thick candles on top of it, and in the middle, on the actual grave, was a mass of inscribed pieces of paper with requests to the Holy Tzadik that he should intercede in Heaven before the Heavenly Father. Some of these little pieces of paper were written in Hebrew, beginning with the name and the mother's name of the petitioner, and asking for family welfare, parnose, or for his wife's and children's health, or his own health, or for children, if the wife was childless (my father must have written hundreds of such petitions before I was finally sent into this world).

In later years I used to visit this old cemetery because there were the graves, in a sort of triptych together, of the fathers of Yiddish literature: I. L. Peretz and his friends Jacob Dineson, one of the earliest novelists I have read with burning interest, and the dramatist and folklorist, S. Anskiu, the author of the Dybbuk.

I left Mr. Silberman's bank and took a tram out to Praga, a big suburb of Warsaw which you passed over the new great bridge which divides Warsaw by the river Vistula from Praga.

The letter I had from Silberman was addressed to the director, Dr. Isaac Schipper, of the Jewish Students home.

I soon gathered from the reception I got from the Secretary that a letter from Pan Silberman meant a great deal to Dr. Schipper, because the banker was one of the chief benefactors of the students' home, being one of the celebrated philanthropists in Warsaw for Jewish and non-Jewish charities. It was said that Silberman donated more than half for the cost of putting up the building – some half a million zlotys – and that he supported it with a yearly grant.

Dr. Schipper was also known to me from the Press, as he was not only a popular deputy in the Polish parliament, but a well-known historian of the Yiddish theatre.

I was immediately put up in a room of my own and did not have to share with other students, mostly poor, who would otherwise have been unable to live in Warsaw and study at the University or do some other academic or literary work. It was a clean, comfortable room with bare walls and a small wooden bed, one table and two chairs, with the window looking over the street – straight over a large gaunt, red brick building, which looked like an old disused prison and was, in fact, the Jewish slaughter house of Praga. I went in there once or twice to watch the killing of oxen, sheep, cows and calves – which made me sick; two or three butcher's assistants held the animal bound on the stone floor, and the *Shokhet* (the Ritual slaughterer) was almost lying on the animal waiting for it to be still, he then cut its throat with a special prescribed instrument – a *Khafet* – which was so razor-sharp that it could cut a hair in the air. I often wondered how this pious looking Jew, with a long curly beard and earlocks, wearing on his head only a *yarmolke*, could have the strength and courage to slaughter a huge struggling ox.

I didn't stay long in the Students Home. I moved to town because it would have taken more than an hour to go to the Bank on Krolewska Street in the centre of Warsaw.

On that Tuesday, the first of March, I started working in the bank. My salary, however, was barely enough to pay for a room and two meals a day in a popular cheap restaurant. The assistant cashier, a short fat man with an enormous grey fringed head, asked me whether I am looking for a room, for as it happened he has one to let in his own house, which is on the Ogrodowa Street, about fifteen minutes from the bank. I told him that I would like to see it and he said to come up after four o'clock, when the bank closes.

I moved in that day with all my belongings – one suitcase. I had a fairly comfortable room, but my window looked out on a blank, dilapidated wall. I had my usual breakfast, rolls and butter, a piece of cheese and coffee, and in the evening a meagre unappetizing dinner.

In the bank I was not happy, on the contrary, I felt a prisoner and that fate has played me a nasty trick. What do I do in a bank sending out reminders that their promissory notes are becoming due on such and such a week, usually a week's notice?

These bills, called *Weksle*, were the only means of exchange known to me. Cheques were rare and most business people paid with such bills of exchange, post-dated sometimes up to six months, which were already endorsed in exchange by a number of firms. I had to write the reminder to the last person on the back side of the bill. I very often made mistakes and whole batches of these cards used to come back as "undelivered", either the street and number were wrong, or the firm was unknown – moved – out of business. I was probably the worst bank clerk there was, and inwardly I think I was proud of my inability to be an efficient member of the bank staff. I was invariably late in the morning, arriving sometimes at half past nine instead of nine o'clock. And why should I be training as a bank clerk when I refused to follow in the footsteps of my father and be a merchant as he had been? I hated all business since the first moment I heard this ugly English word (and I heard it in the bank: Somebody translated to me the phrase "Hours of Business" on a letter, and it sounded to me indecent, for in my ear it translated itself *"businus"* which, in Hebrew means "in Fornication!"

I was dreaming of writing a masterpiece which should, if not change the world, at least bring it a step nearer redemption. Meanwhile I wrote stories and articles of which I was not too proud.

I searched everywhere in the biographies of great writers to see how bad and unhappy they were at uncongenial, commercial jobs. Just a very few years ago I had heard from Dora Dimant that Franz Kafka worked in an Italian Workers Insurance Office in Prague, and was terribly unhappy and bored. Then one day I went downstairs into the basement of the Bank where the records were kept and where a filing clerk was busy searching through old correspondence and big account books, and I saw, over the window with the iron bars beneath the street pavement, a small bird-cage with a yellow canary in it singing away, and, being a hopeless romantic sentimental fool, I took this as an encouraging omen of fate: If a canary can be in a bank cellar, imprisoned in a cage and singing – so can I. And I used to go down there as often as I could to have my lunch of sandwich rolls with tea, supplied by the caretaker.

It was some consolation to see and hear this beautiful bird-prisoner singing away in the cellar of a bank, but I was ashamed to write bad verses about it, and good poetry, alas, I couldn't write. And I was grateful for just knowing the difference. I was afraid to touch poetry since my poor variation on a theme of Dostoyevsky of Christ Jesus before the Spanish Inquisitor who condemned the Jewish Rabbi, with other Jews and Maranos, to be burned on the *Auto da Fe*.

Some days passed at the bank, and I was thinking how to pluck up courage to pay a visit to Julian Tuwim.

CHAPTER EIGHTEEN

One afternoon I took a tram and went to Chlodna Street. It was number four, almost at the corner of Electoralna. I remember so well the address because, not long before, I found a room through an advertisement in a house next to it, number six, on the fourth floor, with a gentle impoverished Jewish family.

I rang Tuwim's bell and a maid opened the door and said that Pan Tuwim is still resting after his lunch, and could I come back in half an hour's time. I went downstairs and marched up and down the street waiting for the half hour to pass.

When I went up again the maid took me straight into Tuwim's study. It was a small, dark room with old fashioned furniture, a desk by the wall with books all round the shelves, on the chairs and the desk, which was also laden with papers.

Tuwim shook hands with me and said: "I just waited for you to call; I wanted to send the letter to Tomaszow." I was wondering what letter he was talking about: "Here it is," he said and took the letter which was standing against the lamp. "I talked to Asch about you, and he was very sympathetic." I opened the envelope and took out the letter which was not sealed. It was short and to the point. It said little about me except that Julian Tuwim had recommended me as an "intelligent and talented" young writer, who would like to get suitable work in Warsaw, and that he would be personally grateful if something could be found for me.

The letter was addressed to Boris Kletzkin, a noted Jewish publisher and a patron of young writers. I was so impressed by this letter that I didn't stay for tea, but left Tuwim and ran down two flights of stairs and took a tram to the Nalewki, the heart of the Jewish quarter in Warsaw.

In the Kletzkin Publishing offices there was also the literary weekly, *Literarishe Bletter*, which was considered a serious magazine.

A big man with a short, well-cut black beard and a naked shining head, came across the office towards me and I recognized him as Boris Kletzkin. I introduced myself and gave him the letter, which he read with raised eyebrows, and said: "Oh! With a recommendation from Asch and Tuwim you *must* be somebody! Come and meet Nachman Maizel, the Editor of the *Literarishe Bletter*." He gave me back the letter and showed me in to Maizel's room. "Show him the letter," he said.

Maizel was behind a desk laden with papers and proofs of the new issue, now in preparation. He was a tall man with quite a handsome face, wavy hair, and a slight stammer.

"Yes!" he said, after glancing through the letter. "It is easy to write such letters, but it isn't easy to find something suitable. However, show something and I'll tell you what I think. I'll see!"

My heart fell, as they say, into my boots. I had imagined that, with a letter from Asch, the portals of literature will open themselves for me. I didn't expect such a reception.

But I later discovered that this was the normal procedure in all Jewish publications, whether on the left or on the right. Well known writers or journalists had difficulties in selling something to the papers, unless he was somebody exceptional. All inside jobs in the Press were taken. There was a crisis in Yiddish book publishing as well.

However, I managed to print a few articles and short stories in one of the two most important newspapers in Warsaw. There were three big national dailies in Warsaw, the *Haint* and *Moment*, and the Socialist daily, by the *Bund*, the *Folkszhytung*. There was also a sensational evening *Express* and an Orthodox paper of the religious Jews, published by the *Aguda*.

When I had my stories published in the *Haint*, where famous writers like Asch, Nahum Sokolow and Zhabotinski used to write, I, myself, began to consider myself as a writer not without promise or talent. And I was flattered when J. Tunkel (who wrote under the pseudonym of "*Der Tunkeler*") complimented me one day in the club of writers and journalists, known as the *Literaten Ferein*, on Tlomazkie Street, Number 13, and said "I've read your story – it's better than mine!"

I was embarrassed; I thought he's making fun of me. Der Tunkeler was the best humourist in Warsaw, and edited a humorous weekly, *Der Krimer Shpigel*.

In the writers' club, I used to meet many of the well-known writers and journalists of the time, who I had heard of or read, for years.

There was also quite a good restaurant there which served traditional Jewish "home cooked" food, and a cold buffet. It was a bit expensive to eat there, but I would allow myself the luxury of lavish food, although I couldn't afford it on my meagre salary, but I used to get some money from my uncle on account of what he owed me for my house.

My boredom and unhappiness in the bank would have been unendurable were it not for the evenings and Saturdays and Sundays I spent there, and, as a budding writer who published in good magazines and newspapers, I was sure that I am on the road to fame.

From time to time I would go to Tomaszow to bask in the glory of my fame. The *Haint* and *Weltshpigel* were read everywhere. Around that time I wrote a long article on *Lion Feuchtwanger* and my editor saved me from a serious embarrassment. I wrote a long review of *Jew Süss* and finished with a paragraph … that never before have I read a book with; such an intimate knowledge and intuition about Jewish life and character and psychological understanding of Jewish history for a non-Jew, as Lion Feuchtwanger's *Jew Süss*." The editor, Jakubuwitz, telephoned me the same day and asked me whether I am out of my mind! … "Since when has Feuchtwanger been a non-Jew?" … And he took out this offending paragraph.

With Jakubuwitz I had rather an amusing incident when I first gave him a story of mine. After giving it to him he asked me to phone him in a few days time.

When I telephoned he asked me to come over to his office, which was in the same building as the *Haint*. I had a premonition that he didn't like my story, so I took with me another short story which I thought might be more to his taste. From a literary point of view it was a much poorer story. I handed it to him and he read it there and then. He had my original story on the desk in front of him, and he said: "Look, your story is not badly written, but the *Weltshpigel* is a family magazine! How can I publish such a story in it?"

At his desk, a crooked smile on his cheek, when he finished reading he said, "Yes. This is very good indeed", And putting it on the cluttered desk added: "This is the kind of story I need." I couldn't help saying, self-satisfactorily; "I told you you'd like it better!" Then he started telling me about his experience as an editor, and he then climbed up a little ladder which stood by the big book-case. He came down with a bound volume of the year's *Weltshpigel*, and said: "I'll show you something." Just have a look at this poem," and he opened a back number somewhere in the volume.

I read the poem and said: "A very original poem." But I didn't know the name of the poet.

"Now," Jakubuwitz said, "I'll tell you a nice story. A couple of weeks ago and I received a letter from an unknown reader saying that I have made a terrible mistake. The poem was not by the undersigned, Yana Kutner, but by no less a poet than Ch. N. Bialik, published several years ago in Odessa. Bialik was then at the height of his fame, both as a Hebrew and Yiddish poet. He lived in Berlin at that time. I wrote a very apologetic letter and begged him to forgive me for my terrible mistake in allowing his poem to appear in my magazine with somebody else's name. And do you know, I received a wonderful letter from Bialik who said that: 'Nothing tragic has happened that I had signed his name under *my* poem. It would have been worse if he had signed *my name* .. under *his* poem…' I liked this story about Bialik's wit but, when I left, it dawned on me that old Yakobovitz told it to me in case my story is also stolen from somebody else …

That year, the first I spent in Warsaw, was quite a happy one. Warsaw had one of the best European theatres and an excellent Opera, as well as a first class philharmonic orchestra, and I never missed an opportunity of seeing a good play and listening to a good concert.

Then a terrible tragedy happened which decided my whole future in the bank.

President Silberman, an indirect victim of the American collapse of the banks, lost a great fortune, or so it seemed to him, and jumped from the 5th. Floor of his apartment … almost exactly like Henryk Landsberg's father some ten years before. He left a widow, a daughter and a young son at Oxford. Mr. Silberman's daughter, Aniuta, a whisp of an elegant girl of twenty-two or three, had just become engaged to Henryk Landsberg. It seemed a strange coincidence of fate that both fathers should have died in such a tragic death.

Horrible as Mr. Silberman's death was (he was just in his early fifties), it also brought back black memories of my father's murder; for as I lost then my protector, I now lost the head of the bank that made my living in Warsaw possible, as I, from the very beginning realised that I was taken into the bank only because he wanted to do a favour to somebody whom Henryk Landsberg was interested. And my fears were realised: A few weeks later I left the bank and went back to Tomaszow where, as a compensation as a minor literary notoriety, it seemed that the whole town, or at least the Jewish population that read the Warsaw National paper, *Der Haint*, has read my stories and they pointed me out in the streets, and some, those who knew me personally, even asked me how it feels to be famous in the Capital.

Little receptions and lectures were organised in town for me. My aunt and uncle insisted that I must not go out to visit anybody: "The whole town," she insisted, "must pay *you* a visit."

But, after Warsaw, Tomaszow looked to me, a little provincial town where you had to wait until noon for the Warsaw papers to arrive, and with only two cinemas where we used to go once a week to both picture houses.

Somehow I arrived in Tomaszow as a kind of envoy of "Literature" and "Love". I had met in the literary club, Z. Segalowidz, one of the most popular writers and poets, who was a steady visitor, and was seen there every day and evenings, walking up and down the big hall with the portraits of Peretz and Sholem Asch on the wall, smoking a huge pipe and looking like an Indian dark prince with his tall thin figure and long, boney olive face. He was always elegantly dressed like an English dandy, and it was rumoured that he had his suits made by one of London's best tailors. What I envied him most was his big briar pipe, and I promptly bought myself one – not so big, but very expensive which I got in an elegant new shop that opened on Krakowskie Pizedmioscie and called itself "*OLD ENGLAND*". It was the best and latest fashion shop for men and, of course, the most exclusive. It was the best and most elegant; it's originality consisted in that the huge shop window had only three items exhibited at one time: One pipe with a white spot on the stem, one silver cigarette lighter, and one tin of pipe tobacco. The moment I had some money to spare I took all my courage in my hands and went in and bought a tin of English pipe tobacco. It was terribly expensive. I opened it according to the instructions on the tin and, in the Club, I, trying to impress Segalowidz with my worldliness, offered him the open tin to take a pipeful. The tobacco in the blue tin was called "*Players Navy Cut*", I asked him why it was called *Navy Cut*. He didn't know. He had never smoked it before; it was too strong, he said.

At home I took an English dictionary and looked up the two words first *Navy*; which seems to mean Fleet, or German *Flotte* and *Cut* means cutting something with a knife, like a piece of bread. But why these two words should have anything to do with pipe smoking – I couldn't understand. Neither could anybody else in the Club.

Segalowidz knew that I came from Tomaszow, and he also knew that I was acquainted with Klara, his mistress, who was the daughter of a Russian Jewish midwife, and was quite a remarkable beauty of the Russian Gypsy type with something Mongolian in her black slit-shaped eyes.

I knew her from several years before, when she was an amateur actress of the local *HaZamir*, the Jewish Choral and Dramatic Society, where I gave my notorious first lecture on Oscar Wilde.

Later, Klara became the librarian of the Socialist Bund Club, where she kept for me, in reserve, the newest books that the Library bought in Warsaw, and it was to me a matter of vain honour to have been the first to have read any newly published book in our town.

When she left the library, she went to try her artistic luck in Warsaw and became, within months, the most talented actress on the Yiddish stage. Warsaw had then the best Yiddish theatre, in the tradition of Esther Kaminska and Jacob Adler to which was added the famous artistic ensemble (Di Viluez Truppe) from Wilno.

Klara, I think, later joined them and became famous after one performance as Leah in the *Dybbuk*.

Segalowidz fell in love with her and they lived together openly, and very soon he married her and took her with him to the Club always. I was glad that she recognised me from her Library days, and invited me to her home.

One Friday I told Segalowidz that I am going for the week-end to Tomaszow.

"Oh!" he said. "You can do something for me: Klara is in Tomaszow and I have got to send her some money. Will you give it to her for me?"

I, of course, was only too pleased to make such a romantic errand, and I put the hundred zloty bills in an envelope.

When I arrived in Tomaszow I went straight to her house, which I knew, and announced my mission. Klara thanked me for my kindness and began reading the letter which I had given her with the money in the envelope. Klara's mother, Mrs. Borodina, a huge shapeless woman with a face like a Cherokee Indian chief, started talking as if to herself: "Last time he was here he didn't speak a word to me. He only said the borsch was too sweet!"

I was very proud of my amorous mission, and thought that I took a minor part as a go-between for the glory of literature and love.

After a few weeks, at the beginning of the new Autumn season, she returned to Warsaw and I saw her very often in the Club. I was not a little pleased when she came over to my table, or asked me to join her. She looked extravagantly beautiful, and wore magnificent clothes, like a first class Warsaw actress, who prided themselves on being as fashionable as actresses of Paris and used distinguished French perfume.

People though, with the exception of Segalowidz, that I too am having an affair with Klara, but I only pretended out of sheer vanity. In truth I was always put off and even frightened by women of the "*Femme Fatale*" type, and she liked to play Nana in real life. I was drawn to more modest beauties, not so ravishing.

I met then two girls in succession, with one of whom I had an affair – at least once a week, but the girl I thought I am really in love with was a student of the Warsaw University, Tania, a classical Jewish beauty with a Madonna face with black big eyes, black fine hair and a delicate olive skin. She was the only daughter of a middle-class Jewish businessman, a timber merchant, and they frightened me considerably; they wanted me to marry their daughter and not just "Go out" with her to theatres and concerts.

But that summer I met a sensible girl, Maryla, who had as much charm and elegance – as she had comfortable proportions! My only fear was that I'd give her a child, and I was just as terrified of getting married to her.

A few months later I got, through my paper, a free passage for two on a Polish Gdynia ship to Sweden.

CHAPTER NINETEEN

We stopped first in Copenhagen, which was the first foreign Capital I had ever seen. I had been dreaming about foreign lands and cities since my boyhood, and here I was in that clean, stately City of Copenhagen, eating the best little sandwiches, which they call smorgasbord, individually packed in paper, and tasting like manna from Heaven. They sold them even in the streets from barrows. I ate the little smorgasbord with relish, and smelt the acid smell of petrol, gasses and fumes from the cars and buses, which was quite a sharper smell than in Warsaw, and being a port it had also the smell of light fog.

I walked the streets of Copenhagen, the town of Kirkegaard of whom I had just heard or read something – "Either/Or", I think. And of *Georg Brandes*, the great Danish critic who was my mentor on European literature.

Brandes real name was Cohen, and his brother was the editor of *Politiken*, Denmark's most respected paper. I remember *Politiken* for another reason; we were received there with a group of foreign journalists by the editor and staff – and we were served CHAMPAGNE with the delicious smorgasbord. That was the first time I had ever tasted champagne; it had a peculiar, indescribable taste, but the name CHAMPAGNE had a most potent magic of which we had read in the French and Russian novels, where rich lovers drank the Champagne from the slippers of their mistresses and courtesans.

A year later I had the opportunity to go to the Scandinavian countries a second time. On a free boat voyage, and also I had a three months' rail ticket from Stockholm up to *Riksgrantsen* on the

Norwegian border in the far North. The journey by boat from Nord through the Fiords to Bergen was the first magnificent sea voyage I ever made. And, as usual, I identified with genius, and saw in my mind's eye Henryk Ibsen, travelling on such a boat to the little fishing town of Bergen, hidden in the mountains, which you can reach with a funicular railway. I had a strange fascination for Ibsen, read his plays (in a bad Yiddish translation), and saw several of his more famous plays acted in Warsaw.

Besides, I had something remotely in common with old Henryk. I, too, was an assistant in an Apothecary and tried to learn the trade of pharmacy as a first step to learn Latin, and, perhaps, medicine.

When I returned to Warsaw, I published a few travel sketches and short stories and became known as an "expert" on Scandinavian countries, and a "World traveller", because the travel bug (the wanderlust) got into my bones, and I began dreaming incessantly about seeing the whole World. Vienna, Prague (which from the time I met Dora Dimant became to me the City of Kafka), and the mystical *Maharal's Golem*; I dreamed of Berlin and Paris and, oh, of course, Rome.

Every year the Catholic Churches in Warsaw organised pilgrimages of the faithful to Rome, and I remember how desperately I wanted to take part in such a pilgrimage, although I knew that, as a Jew, I would be automatically excluded even if I had had the money to pay for the fare. London was so far removed, so enveloped in fog and mystery, that I could only think of nineteenth-century England at its most strange as seen in the mirror of Dickens, which I only knew from Polish and Yiddish translations. London was so far away that, looking at the map, I thought of as an ultime thule, the last country on the northern top of Europe. My dreams of England began when a quiet drama, to me a great tragedy, occurred, when my most romantic love, Adela, went away to London where she had a brother. I was then still, of course, in Tomaszow and my misery was so great at her departure that I thought I'll never see her again, that I am losing her for ever. She was away in London for one year (and I got from her only one post-card!), and I kept on imagining that the Prince of Wales, whom we thought the most handsome and elegant man in the world, will see her and will fall in love with her. How I came to think so much of the Prince of

Wales (whom we called in Polish, Ksiezna Walji), and associated him as a model for my friend, the rich and fashionable Henryk Landsberg, the leader of the "golden youth", I shall never know.

But after a year Adela came back to Tomaszow, and I must admit that deep in my soul I was pleased that the Prince of Wales had not fallen in love with her. But so mysterious are the ways and fortunes of love that, when she came back, I was no longer so insanely in love with her. There was another girl, Cesia, the younger sister of Meir and Roza, the dedicated members of the Communist party, who did illegal work for the movement.

Just after Adela came back I had suddenly an idea that I must learn the English language from her, as she prided herself that she can speak the language fluently. She advised me what books to buy and I remember one big one, *English for Polish Students*. And she started giving me lessons once a week. It was hard going and I had trouble with the strange vocabulary, particularly with the extraordinary spelling. The first word I remember that struck me as downright preposterous was the word "Church"– pronounced *Jchertsh*– to this day I read "Khurtche" whenever I see Church written. Russian we were used to, Polish we knew, German we knew, even French we often heard spoken, but we never heard English spoken, and it sounded downright Tartarish, and we didn't believe that English children could possibly learn to spell and pronounce it.

Once, in the train on the way to Warsaw, I was sitting in a compartment of the third class, and just in front of me was a notice advertising that a regular shipping line of the *Gydnia* had been opened which leaves once every week from the port of Gydnia to London, with a big picture of the ship. I noted down the address and made a silent vow to myself that I must go and see London. I had dreamed of London so much that I sometimes thought I had been there in a former life. But I had only the conventional picture of London Bridge, the Tower of London and the Houses of Parliament.

On arrival in Warsaw I wrote to the Shipping Company and proposed that I shall write a series of travel articles if they will give me a free passage. I also promised them free advertisements in my provincial newspaper of Tomaszow.

And … lo and behold … within a few weeks I got a letter from the Head of the Shipping Company in Gdynia, with two tickets on their ship, *Poniatowski* to London. You can imagine my rejoicing! But this was only half of my worries. The biggest problem was how to get an English visa. This was the greatest nightmare; for everywhere you heard and read in the newspapers how difficult, almost impossible, it was to get visas to Palestine, and still more miraculous to get a visa to England.

England was a closely guarded and small island. (By some strange association I remember somebody squeezing himself into a packed Synagogue and saying facetiously: "This is not a Synagogue … this synagogue is England." In Yiddish "England" means literally "Tight Land!") And since then the association of the two words "Eng" and "Tight" had stayed with me, and I couldn't think of England otherwise than as a little packed island, brimful of people, and even now, whenever I have the chance of travelling through the English countryside, I am amazed at the vast lands and forests that you see – without a single human habitation.

To emigrate, to leave, to escape from Poland, was the dream of everyone of the young people I knew or heard of. Poland was then engulfed by anti-Semitic waves, coming from the Government and the middle classes, as well as from the workers and peasants. The military, the Government of the Colonels, and the Catholic Press, carried on a campaign against the whole Jewish population which numbered over three and a half million Jews, mostly small shop keepers and artisans. A few big industrial enterprises and Banks were run by Jews, who wanted to be accepted as Poles, and many of them were converts to Catholicism. Jews were squeezed out from the economy by high taxation and open boycott. "Swoj do swego" – (*everyone to his own*) were slogans you could see on Jewish shops everywhere. *Zydzi do Palestiny – Jews to Palestine!* And *Nie Kap n Zyuda,* "Don't buy from a Jew." In the smaller towns, in Bialystock, in Rodom, in the Poznan districts, the soldiers or organized bands of hooligans killed, here and there Jewish families, many travellers who looked Jewish were thrown out of running trains, long grey beards were torn out from old men, and, only in more merciful cases, were the beards cut with knives or bayonets.

Hundreds of thousands of Jews wanted to emigrate and they flocked to the consulates in Warsaw: Palestine, the Promised Land, was closed, and there were only a few certificates for the great number who applied for their permits to go to America – the new Promised Land – which had a very low quota, and only the lucky ones had relatives already in the States, who could support them and send them a "*Shif's Karte*", a ship ticket, could hope to go there.

The idea of my being able to go to London, and even take someone with me, was so remote that I was afraid to go to the British Consulate in Warsaw – almost certain that they would refuse to give me a visa. And when I finally went there I remember a curious little incident. When I arrived (I forget now where the street was), the gate of the visa department was closed, and I rang the bell. A man in civilian clothes came out and said: "Can't you read? Don't you see that the visa department is closed from one to three o'clock? What's the use of ringing?"

I saw the strength of his argument, and at the same time it dawned on me that this is the *British* Consulate: And when it said "*Closed*" it meant just that – and there was no arguing with them! Greater was my surprise that when I came back the man asked me in Polish what I intended to do in London. I wrote down my profession on the form I was given, the official looked through it, and finally said: "One pound sterling" (some sixty zlotys, if I remember rightly). The man took the form and entered a neighbouring room; he came back within minutes – with my visas stamped on my passport: good for "two weeks" stay in England!

Now I had the problem of whom among my friends and colleagues to take with me to London.

I first thought of Julian Tuwim. He was then engaged in the famous Warsaw Review Theatre, *Qui Pro Quo*. Tuwim was not only the finest poet in Poland, but was also admired greatly for his Satires and burlesque sketches in the *Qui Pro Quo*. He came out immediately to see me and, with his famous satirical smile, he told me that he would have liked to go with me to London, only unfortunately he can't go by boat – he suffers from terrible sea-sickness, even from a short excursion on the river Vistula. He was very sorry, and thanked me sincerely for my suggestion. I was disappointed but had to accept his genuine excuse. Tuwim was not only the most famous and most widely read poet but, together with Antony Slonimski, he became the subject of a heated discussion in the daily Press, particularly the anti-Semitic newspapers of the extreme Catholic right. And anti-Semitic hooligans attacked both of them, Tuwim and Slonimski, in the "*Mala Ziemianska*" (a café by that name) where writers, artists and journalists used to meet in the afternoons for a "*pol czarnej*" (half a glass of black coffee). They were both belaboured and kicked about, sustaining wounds over their heads, and called "Zydo Masoin Komuna" (Jewish Masonic Communists – the usual epithet for a Jewish intellectual, even if he was a known anti-Communist, as Tuwim and Slonimski were).

We talked about these attacks, and suddenly Tuwim said to me, with a shade of melancholy in his voice, "You know, I envy you!" I wondered, surprised, what he could envy in me, an almost unknown writer.

"You have," he said, "at least your own language. I write in a language *in which they curse me!*" He underlined, as it were, the last phrase. That the greatest poet of the Polish language should envy me, a beginning Yiddish writer, moved me deeply. The bitter irony of it all!

I left him with a heavy heart, but with all my poverty in speaking and writing in a minority language, I nevertheless felt a certain pride that I have not forsaken the language of my ancestors, like Tuwim, and of not trying to become a "real" Pole.

From Tuwim I went to the Literary Club to see if I can find somebody whom I could take with me on my second ticket to London. I met there J. J. Trunk, a writer of great talent and erudition. He was not only of a famous Chassidic family, whose grandfather was one of the illustrious Polish Rabbis, but also a very wealthy man, and a member of the Jewish Socialist Party, The Bund. He was a lovable eccentric man who told stories with such comic facial expressions, mostly stammering, that they had a hilarious effect. He also translated Gilgamesh into Yiddish. I used to meet him at Klara Segalowidz's with other writers, like the celebrated H. D. Nomberg, who was also a popular representative in the Polish *Sejm* (Parliament) of the Jewish *Folk's* – People's Party. Trunk told me that he wouldn't be able to go because his wife was not well.

So I went to Nachman Maisil, the Editor of the (Literziski)? *Literashzi Bletter* the best literary weekly published in Yiddish. Maisil was a critic and belonged to the group of Russian Jewish writers who came to Warsaw, after the Russian Revolution, from Kiev, together with the novelist David Bergelson and Peretz Markisch (probably the best Yiddish writer of the time). It was to Maisil that I went with the letter of recommendation from Sholem Asch. Markisch was undoubtedly the most vociferous, talented and revolutionary Yiddish poet. He was also extremely handsome, with a beautiful head with wild, black locks, and conquering eyes. Warsaw women went, as the saying goes, "crazy" about him and when he visited the provinces, with a lecture and recital of his poetry, which was organized by the *Literashzi Bletter* that had a rostrum of writers and poets who read their works and turned into lecturers who filled theatres or Halls at 10 o'clock in the morning with an enthusiastic public, that was carried away with revolutionary enthusiasm.

Markisch, who I talked to several times, spoke Yiddish with a strong Russian accent, and with a warm, delightful intimacy, as if he had known you all his life. He was the most enthusiastic Communist, although I don't know whether he was a member of the illegal Polish Communist Party.

But he certainly was their best known and unpaid propagandist. He was joined by a number of other writers, especially *David Bergelson*, probably the most representative of the modern Jewish novelists coming from Russia. He lived with his wife for a few years after the Revolution in Berlin, where his wife, I believe, worked as an official in the Soviet Embassy. Bergelson and Markisch had nothing but scorn and hatred, but no pity, for the non-political Yiddish writers who wrote for the bourgeois, Zionist, or even Bundist Socialist Press. Zionism, in particular, was to them an instrument, or rather a "lackey" of British Imperialism, and the Bundists and other social democrats they called *Social-Fascists*. The Soviet Union was the only Fatherland of the World proletariat, where Stalin's new Constitution solved the Jewish problem in Russia. There is no more anti-Semitism, as the great Lenin had predicted, under the dictatorship of the proletariat.

I am telling all this and, at the same time, begging the reader to allow me to anticipate: Years later, after the Hitler War, Stalin had them all murdered, together with the best Jewish writers, poets and artists, among them Peretz Markisch, David Bergelson, Itzek Feffer, Vovsi Michaels (the actor, founder and director of the Moscow Jewish Art's Theatre, the best modern theatre in the Jewish world), and a host of others whom I didn't know personally. A few years earlier Isaac Babel died a miserable death in a concentration camp ("lucky were those who were just shot" – supposed to have said a great Russian Jewish poet, Mandelstam, who died in a Labour camp in Siberia).

I didn't know Babel, but I once asked Ilia Ehrenberg, when he visited Warsaw, who was the greatest Russian writer? And his answer was Isaac Babel; And the most important poet? – Pasternak, he said.

At about that time my friend Hela Ashkenazy, a teacher of French, who studied at the Sorbonne, a woman of great culture and a vivacious warm personality, took me under her wings and tried to implant some kind of French culture into me and taught me the great French classics. She believed in my little talent and expected something of me in the future. She treated me as Madame de Waren treated Rousseau, although there was no love affair between us.

However, she admonished me severely and screamed at me for being so lazy and imagining myself a writer only having published a few short stories and articles.

"What do you imagine," she shouted – almost in irony – at me, "that you'll go through life, swinging your cane and being a dandy, and buying yourself elegant ties and suits, and believing yourself to be a Tuwim or Baudelaire?" She was very stern with me, yet, in her way, she liked me and even had faith in me. I loved her great intelligence and took her as a real mother figure. But this didn't help me; the man who loved her and wanted to marry her, was jealous of me whenever he found me in her flat. His name was B. Shefner and he was one of the best publicists and satirists in Warsaw. He wrote exclusively for the Bundist paper, Folkszeitung, whose editor was Henryk Ehrlich, the leader of the Social Democratic Bundist Party. He was a tall distinguished man, with a little yellow beard and friendly, blue eyes. Ehrlich was respected and admired even by his political enemies of both right and left. He was famous as the Socialist lawyer who defended Communists at the Warsaw Bar. A first class leader-writer and public speaker, he was also a member of the Warsaw County Council, and fought valiantly with the reactionary leaders of the *ENDEKS* (the National Democrats), whose policy was – like the Government's, to squeeze the Jews out of trade and industry, making their economic and cultural life intolerable, and force them to emigrate from Poland.

There were about three and a half million Jews dwelling in Poland, for they dwelt more than they lived. The poverty was shameful. Half the Jewish population were workers, traders, small shop-keepers, artisans, and market Jews (so called) who kept stalls on the two market days, Tuesdays and Fridays, in the towns.

I, am not quoting statistics, but it was believed that there were also many thousands, so it was said, of rich Jewish property owners, manufacturers, especially in our town and in Lodz and Warsaw, and Bankers, private financiers, and common petty money-lenders who lent money to the poor and were called "procentniks", usurers, whom everybody despised – including the Jews.

There were a great number in the academic professions; doctors, lawyers, engineers and, on rare occasions, a Jewish professor. There was a strict *Numerus Clausus* for Jewish students, which limited the attendance of the Jewish students, as well as the Faculty members being openly anti-Semitic. I saw at the Universities of Warsaw and Wilno Jewish students standing, rather than sitting down on separate benches – the first kind of "apartheid" – and many Jewish students clamoured to leave for the universities of Berlin, Paris, Vienna, Prague and Montpelier. Some went to Italy or Belgium and Holland. Few, somehow, went to England, except the sons of the rich and the aristocracy. Most students were desperately poor. They were sons of artisans, of the proletariat, or small shop-keepers and tailors and shoemakers, whose only hope in the world was that their sons will be doctors, and escape the tribulations, the animosity and the insecurity of the poor Jew. It must be remembered that in Poland, as formerly in Russia before the Revolution, doctors belonged to the privileged class of the intelligentsia, who were not only respected, but admired and venerated by all the people, Jews and Gentiles alike. Religious

Jews believed that with every doctor riding in a carriage to visit a patient, an angel rides by his side, whether he is a Jewish or a Christian doctor, and it was customary in the street – when a doctor passed by – to greet him by removing one's hat, and which greeting the doctor answered by waving his hand like Royalty, or a Cardinal!

The doctors were so called leaders of the intelligentsia, but mostly of the right bourgeoisie, then came the lawyers, the chemists (apothecaries), the dentists and photographers, (who belonged to the Arts intelligentsia, and considered themselves "artists" together with painters and musicians). Then there were the so called intelligentsia of the Left: The Socialists, the Labour Zionists, the illegal Communists, who worked among the proletariat in the factories and had their eyes turned towards Moscow, and obeyed the political directives and party line. There was a constant inter-party struggle, sometimes violent, at political meetings and street marchings. But all of them, without distinction, attacking Polish Catholic anti-Semitic, who hated them all no matter to which party they belonged, and, strange to say, that among the attackers were not only the Polish riffraff and hooligan monsters, but many university students took part in beating up Jewish students. I, and the rest of us, lived in constant fear and trembling, with the exception of the so-called *Assimilated* Jews (known as Poles of the Mosaic Religion), who tried to be more Polish than the Poles, and some went over to Catholicism and inter-married, hiding from their offspring the dark secret of their Jewish descent.

One of those converted Jews was the eminent poet and critic Antoni Slonimski, a close friend of Tuwim who would not – or could not – hide his Jewish wit and irony. I went to see him for an interview after he was badly attacked by a group of anti-Semitic officers for criticising the fascist and reactionary tendencies of the leaders of the Government. He was accused of unpatriotic and left sympathies.

Slonimski was famous for another reason, not only for his satirical writings but for the fact that he was the grandson of the famous leader of the Jewish *Enlightenment*, the *Haskala*, Haim Selig Slonimski, the man who first founded and edited the first *Ha-Tsfira*, a daily newspaper in Warsaw in the Hebrew language, and published popular scientific books on mathematics, History and Science, in books which became popular both with the religious youth and intelligentsia, who turned from orthodoxy to Enlightenment.

Slonimski used to write regularly in the *Wladomosei Literackie* and was read by the whole Polish and Jewish intelligentsia, and although the majority of readers of such intellectual periodicals were Jewish, as were the music lovers and book readers, Slonimski would sometimes come out with satirical remarks about his own Jewish readers – who resented it greatly. When I visited him in this flat, I mentioned this to him and told him that some Jewish readers resent his ironical sounding remarks, which seemed to them anti-Semitic.

"Well", he answered, "I have always been an anti-Semite. I have always been "Anti" – and always "Semitic" …"

I published my article in the *Haint* and, about the same time, I made an appointment with Poland's leading anti-Semitic writer, who happened to have been a very talented publicist and witty theatre critic, Adolf Nowaczynski. A few years before he had published a big volume, in a yellow paper-back of about 1000 pages, an Anthology of Anti-Semitic writings. This was a collection of the grossest forgeries, lies and calumnies from ancient sources down to modern times, about the conspiracy of the Jews to conquer the world – something on the lines of the notorious forgeries of the "*Wise Men of Zion*". I bought a copy and read it practically the whole way through. From my earliest youth I was deeply interested in Anti-Semitics, and I hoped one day to write a history of anti-Semitism.

I remember once talking to an old scholar, who used to come up from time to time to the Literary Club, Szapiro was his name. Once I sought his advice and asked him if he can help me with a bibliography of anti-semitica.

"Read Jewish history," he answered, "and you'll have the history of Anti-Semitism."

I decided I shall go and ask Adolf Nowaczynski for an interview. Perhaps from him I might learn about the true sources of anti-Semitism.

I went up to his study to see him. He received me with old Polish politeness, and asked me to sit down beside his big mahogany desk.

He was a man in his early fifties and had a common, though not unpleasant, face.

We started talking about his Anti-Semitic *"Wise Men of Zion"*. But, as with many an anti-Semite, he assured me that he has never been a Jew hater – and that "Some of my best friends are Jews." He appreciates the Jewish genius, and knows many Jews have made great contributions to culture, but Poland has too many Jews, and they occupy too many prominent places in banking, industry and the professions. He agreed with the Minister, Grabski's slogan; he, the Minister of Pilsudski's Government, had said in a speech in the *Sejm*, that he is against the forcible expulsion of Jews from Poland, but was for an economic boycott and orderly emigration – *Owswem!* – of course! Afterwards this "Owszem" became an anti-Jewish slogan among Jews and Poles.

When I came to the editor of the, *Haint*, Mr. Goldberg, he read it in front of me, and lifted his eyes up to me from the manuscript (making no secret that he liked it) and asked: "What will I do if he (Nowaczynski) denies it?" "I shall answer him," I said promptly, "that he is lying!" He was satisfied with my reply.

A few days later I went into the editor's office of the *Haint* and met there, sitting by Goldberg's chair, Sholem Asch. I had never seen him before. He had the letter of recommendation about me from Julian Tuwim. I introduced myself and he remembered: "If Tuwim spoke well of you, you must have talent," he said, and he asked me to accompany him to his hotel. He called a carriage outside the office and asked the driver to take us to the Hotel Europejski, where he was staying.

"So, you are doing well I see?" he said. He was sure that the fact that my short stories appeared in the Haint was thanks to his letter, and I didn't want to disappoint him. Sholem Asch was, by reputation, the most powerful writer of his time. He was a protégé of the greatest neo-classical writer, Peretz. It was to him that he first went with his romantic short novel *Das Shtetl* – (The Little Town), an idealized picture of a small Jewish provincial town in Poland, with all its joys and sorrows. This little book was a short epic and created a whole literature which tried, unsuccessfully, to recapture Asch's nostalgia for the pious, hard and dangerous life in the Polish small towns. He had a host of imitators, and was loved, envied and hated for his phenomenal success in Poland, and translated very early into foreign languages. He also made a name for himself by his dramatic works which were produced in Moscow and in Berlin, under the direction of the rising star of European directors, Max Rheinhardt, which was the highway to success.

He was, in a word, the first Yiddish writer to achieve international fame, which grew and grew to the end of his life in London. He was an impressive figure of a man, very tall, over six foot, with a handsome head that looked more like an athlete's head than that of an intellectual. He had big black eyes, and a round self-satisfied face, always well shaven and smelling of eau-de-cologne. He wore expensive clothes and elegant ties, and hand-made silk or linen shirts which, it was said, his wife ordered for him. Yet he had a reputation of being a mean, miserly and vain man.

A secretary of his once told me that Asch is the most egotistical man he had ever known. He would spend on himself fortunes and would not help a colleague in need. He was a thoroughly selfish man, never giving a thought to anybody but himself. When he would come to Warsaw (he spent the 1914-18 war years in America and became an American Citizen. He built himself a house in the South of France, and he had an apartment in Paris), he behaved as a rich but mean American "uncle" towards his fellow writers, most of whom were poor and had to supplement their incomes by hackwork journalism. He expected his arrival in Warsaw to be announced on the front pages of the daily Press, and the extraordinary thing was that the Jewish papers did carry huge headlines whenever he arrived or appeared publicly at a political or literary meeting in Warsaw or Lodz.

There were numerous stories going around about his miserliness. I experienced a few myself. The first was when I travelled with him in the carriage, and we stopped at the most expensive hotel in Warsaw, the *Europejski*; he asked me to pay the driver, knowing very well that I have little money. When we were in his elegant hotel room, and the waiter brought up a drink, he asked me to tip the man. He had "no change" he said!

He had a habit of not recognizing or forgetting the names of people that he really knew well in the past, or contorting their names. Once, I remember, he came up to the Literary Club and met there one of the best writers who he knew from early days. His name was *Ephraim Kaganowski*. I knew Kaganowski very well, and he was known, not only as one of the best short-story writers, but as a sharp ironic wit. Asch saw him and greeted him with: "How are you *Kaganowicz*?"

"Not so bad, Mr. Aschenberg!" Kaganowski replied, and walked out of the room.

Asch was always suspicious that the poor writers will try to borrow money from him, so he forestalled them by telling them about his financial worries, and how exaggerated it was that he is well off; really – he is a poor man with vast expenses, a wife, a daughter for whom he must buy expensive clothes and jewellery … Besides … he has two grown-up sons who constantly ask him for money … they don't earn a penny between them … one even chose to become a writer (would you believe it?) … in England! Also, he cant dismiss his secretary, who without him would have starved. And what about his own family? Constantly asking him to support them? Years later I met Asch in London at the famous jeweller Moshe Oved, whose jewellery shop was at the corner of New Oxford Street, and was called "*Cameo Corner*" (about whom I shall have something to say later on). Moshe Oved's customers were an international clientele of world famous Hollywood Stars and great personalities of the great aristocracy, and the not so aristocratic American millionaires. But his most honoured customer was Her Majesty Queen Mary and all the British Royal family patronized his shop. Queen Mary used to buy from him all her jewellery which she gave as gifts at Christmas etc. She loved, he told me, bargains, and Moshe Oved, to please her would give her the lowest prices … more often than not below cost price.

One day I saw Asch there. He greeted me as if he remembered me from Warsaw. He looked at various pieces of Italian Renaissance jewellery. Moshe Oved told me that a few weeks before he had shown him a very costly, ancient Greek Intaglio ring, worth a lot of money, and Asch came running the next morning, as soon as the shop was opened, and almost cried that he should give him that ring. "I can't write without the ring! … I dreamed that I finished my new novel with that ring on my finger, but when I woke up I couldn't write a word without the ring! I dreamed that the ring was made especially for me. For the sake of Jewish literature you must not deny me that ring! I shall never write again without it. Do you want to be responsible for such a catastrophe?"

Moshe Oved had to give him the ring which was some 2500 years old, and worth a small fortune.

A week or so later I visited Asch in his London hotel. We had tea with his young daughter and her fiancé. I knew her from Warsaw when she was a teenager, and I made some facetious remark, using a common hackneyed phrase: "I remember you when you were young and innocent …" (meaning simply that I have known her years ago when she was an adolescent). Asch, whose English was appalling, felt immediately that I have insulted his daughter in front of her fiancé, turned his back on me during tea-time and wouldn't say another word to me.

Next morning, when I rang him up, he answered the telephone, and when he heard my voice he simply said: "I don't want to speak to you …!" and banged down the phone. Although I knew that he was a boorish man, I couldn't understand his tactless behaviour and I couldn't understand what crime I had committed to merit such treatment from him.

It was Moshe Oved who told me that Asch is mad at me for insulting his daughter in front of her fiancé. It then dawned upon me that my colloquial phrase (which Asch had probably heard for the first time) .. "When you were young and innocent …") had taken it literally.

Weeks later when I met him at Moshe Oved's Cameo Corner, he deigned to nod his head to me … as if he had forgiven me for my *terrible* faux pas. It was the beginning of winter and a mild day. Asch, who was always dressed in an American flashy style, was wearing an expensive sable overcoat, and I was fool enough to let him know that in England only foreigners wear fur coats; that it is very un-English for men to dress like that.

Asch promptly answered me back: "Why does the English King

wear a fur-coat then?" I said something to the effect that the King is an old man and has to be careful, and Asch came back at me with a venomous folksy Yiddish expression: "He who has one … wears it, and he who hasn't .. *ligt in der erd* (is buried in the earth) …" He had such a vulgar trait in his character with his great talent. Incidentally, he was the only writer whom I read as a youth and cried reading it. It was "*KIDDUSH HASHEM*", his novel of the great Jewish Massacres in the Ukraine in the years 1648–1649.

Chapter Twenty

Meanwhile I prepared myself for the exciting journey into that mysterious land, England, but deep in my heart I buried a secret which I dared not even believe myself in it's reality: I shall never come back to Poland again! Enough of the humiliation, the fear and trembling; the mean and murderous anti-Semitism, and above all, the terrible murder of my father when my mother and I could as easily have been killed in seconds, as he was for no reason at all.

I loved Poland. I thought it a beautiful country, rich in grain, fruit, and with its golden fields in summer and even green or white trees stretching for miles on the roads, with a crucifix or portrait of the Madonna at the cross-roads. I loved the Tatra Mountains and Zakopane, the Winter resort covered in snow on top of the high mountains, although, when I first climbed with a party and guide one of the highest mountains near the lake *Morskie Oko*, on the other side of which you can see the valley of Czechoslovakia, I had to crouch on my hands and knees, and made a vow that if ever I became a millionaire I'll abolish mountain climbing – and even mountains!

But now I was preparing myself for the most exciting journey of my life to that unknown, remote island, England, shrouded in mist and mystery. I left Poland as one leaves a wicked step-mother.

My companion was Noel Maisil, the editor of the *Literashzi Bletter*, where I was beginning to publish a few literary reviews. He was delighted with the free passage to England and back, and he even suggested (which I secretly hoped for) that he will pay my hotel bill in exchange for his free passage.

I got my visa a week or two earlier. I had postponed going to the British Embassy for weeks, being afraid that they would refuse me a visa: Whom am I, to want to go to England? A journalist? Yes! But have you enough money to live in England? I might just as well ask for a visa to Eldorado. I knew hundreds of people and heard tragic stories of people who couldn't get visas to Palestine … let alone England. But, as I related earlier, my fears were ungrounded and I got my visas with no trouble at all – except having to wait for the two hours when they were closed.

Our ship was only a cargo boat, and carried, besides me, only two or three other passengers. We dined with the Captain in his large dining-room which looked like a cottage, with a big oak table, but the food was excellent. Our Polish chef served us a dish which is called in Poland "*Zrazy a la Nelson*", and which we took for a good omen on our way to Nelson's country.

For breakfast I had for the first time kippers which, the Captain informed us, is typically British. I liked it from the first mouthful. Funny, I thought, we have salt herring and the English practically never taste it … and they have kippers which are unknown to us.

We went through the Kiel Canal and when we approached the docks of London it was the fourth day of our misty sea journey.

I knew that we had reached London by the yellow fog, which the English called a "pea-soup" fog. Never had I seen such a yellow fog, and when I read Dickens (in a bad translation), I didn't believe that such a thing really existed.

When I stood at the Passport Control the officer, in civilian clothes, asked me how long I want to stay. I said: "Two," meaning two weeks … but I forgot the words! "Oh! Two months," said the man, and stamped my passport.

When we talked out in to the fog there stood a policeman in a dark blue half-cape, before whom I took off my hat, just as a sign of respect. I could hardly make out his face in the fog, he stood enveloped in a yellow cloud.

Maisil had an address of a cheap hotel in Aldgate, and we took a taxi and landed at a third-class, Jewish owned, hotel called Central, at the corner of Mansell Street and Aldgate, almost in the heart of the East End and Whitechapel. The Hotel, although fairly clean, had that typical Jewish smell of good Jewish food, the only pleasant, but strange smell came from the fried plaice and cod, sea-food which we never had in Poland.

After unpacking, we strolled out into the fog to play a visit to the two Yiddish newspapers, "The JEWISH TIMES", called *The Tzait* in Whitechapel, and to the *Jewish Post*, just around the corner in Davies Street. They seemed very pleased to see us and treated us as celebrated Jewish writers from Poland, but asked us how long we intended to stay. We knew that compared to Jewish Warsaw London was a backward and provincial town, as far as Jewish culture was concerned. The two papers, both dailies, had a struggle to keep alive, and it was said that if a Jew died ... they lost a reader. There was no immigration from Eastern Europe, and the generation of Yiddish readers diminished year by year ... almost month by month.

The first thing they asked us was how long we intend to stay. Maisil said he is going back in a week; I hesitated, and then said that I was going to remain. They were horrified and both editors advised me strongly against such a reckless decision: "There is nothing happening in London, and for a young writer Jewish London is a desert. There is no cultural life whatsoever."

Maisil himself was aghast at my answer that I intended to stay on in London: "Why?" he said. "You'll starve here. In Warsaw you're already getting to be known, but here you'll starve!" I said that I'd prefer to starve in London than go back to Warsaw. I wanted first to learn English and get to know The Mysterious land and people, which had become almost a passion with me. I decided to stay ... come what may.

Maisil had two more addresses; one was the painter Pilichowski, who was born in Poland and made a name for himself there as an academic painter of a Jewish guise, he was also a friend of Sholem Asch, and an admirer of Jewish literature. He left Poland early for Germany and then settled in England where he painted many portraits of the aristocratic and wealthy classes. But his later fame rested on an historical painting of the opening of the Hebrew University in Jerusalem, with Lord Balfour (of the famous *Balfour Declaration* of the British Government to create a National Home for the Jews in Palestine) in Academic gown, standing in the middle among a huge number of Zionists and other celebrities, among whom were Professor Chaim Weitzman, Nahum Sokolow, Usishkin, Bialik, and other famous men and women of English society. This group – or mass portrait – became universally wide-spread in the Jewish world as an epoch making picture, and the dawn of a new era for the Jewish People. In Polish Jewish homes, I remember, it was hung on the walls, and there was hardly a house which did not display it, and it was no less popular in other Eastern European countries where Lord Balfour was looked upon as a new fore-runner of the coming Messiah, and the British Government as messengers of *Redemption* of the Jewish people.

When we visited Pilichowski in his home off Abbey Road in St. John's Wood, he received us with great old-world courtesy. He gave us tea with excellent cakes and offered us a drink of *aqua vitae*. He then took us to his large studio where he kept his huge painting under a cover. The painting had already been known to us from the innumerable copies that had been reproduced all over the world – especially in Jewish communities. But I was not impressed by it as a work of art, more as an historical document.

Naturally we complimented him on his important achievement, and we asked him to show us some of his latest paintings. He did so with enthusiasm; he expected us to be impressed – and we didn't disappoint him! It was easy … because Maisil understood nothing about art, and wouldn't have known the difference between a Rembrandt and a Pilichowski. Later on an art critic, who was also a good literary critic, Leo Koenig (who was to become a close friend of mine), told me that there are rumours that Pilichowski painted in many heads of ladies and gentlemen of the Anglo-Jewish society who were never actually present at the great event.

From his studio in the garden, he took us back to his big drawing-room, magnificently furnished in heavy oak, with huge comfortable deep arm-chairs. On the walls were hanging some of his early works and also an Italian early Renaissance master, whom I didn't know.

He treated us to his reminiscences, of his beginnings in Poland,

and later in Germany and Paris, where he became a friend of Sholem Asch and other writers and artists who later became famous.

Pilichowski was in his sixties, but still robust, with a face of a Jewish artisan with Polish, peasant, blue eyes, shining with good nature. His hair, now greying, must once have been blond. He did not advise me to go back to Poland when Maisil told him of my intention to remain in London.

It was agreed that I should write down a series of interviews with him for the *Literarishe Bletter* in Warsaw, which would consist mainly of his reminiscences of artists and writers, as well as political Zionist leaders, like Weitzman, Sokolow and Nordau.

When I visited him alone, a week or so later in his studio and taking notes, he asked me where I am staying, and when I told him that as long as Maisil is with me we were staying in an hotel in Aldgate, but I was in a quandary where to live after Maisil leaves London. I assured him that I did not intend to go with him and had made up my mind not to return to Poland, although I had a return ticket on the same boat which brought us to London.

"Then," he said, "we must find you somewhere to live." And immediately he got up and telephoned the Director of the Jewish Shelter, which was a charitable institution supported by the Jewish Board of Guardians which was built especially to house immigrant Jews, mostly Russian and Polish, or those who were in transit for America. He told them that I was a young Jewish writer from Poland who deserves to be put up immediately. He also apparently said some nice things about me, which I only guessed at because my English was very poor, although in the two weeks I had managed to read a few books and a lot of newspapers to practice this forbidding language.

We talked for over two hours, and he gave me a standing invitation to come to Friday evening and Saturday lunch, which Sabbath days he kept surrounded by his family in the traditional way. Before I left he took me aside and put some money in my pocket, and said: "You can't go about without money in London!" Embarrassed at the two half-crowns he had given me, I nevertheless thanked him kindly for the thought, and left.

I went straight by bus to Aldgate, which I already knew because there, in the same building, was the Jewish Art Society, the Ben Uri Gallery, with a permanent exhibition of Jewish artists and which was also some kind of Cultural and Literary Society. It was here that a reception was given for Maisil and myself, two "distinguished" writers from Poland, a few days before, under the chairmanship of the President of the Ben Uri who was also one of it's benefactors. This man was Edward Good, an original character whose name and address I knew from Poland.

Edward Good (originally Goodak), who later changed his name to Moshe Oved (the Servant), was an antique jeweller, and wrote verse and prose. He invited me to come to his antique jewellery shop at Cameo Corner in New Oxford Street; a little shop which was a small museum of rare gold rings, Greek, Roman, Etruscan, Egyptian and Renaissance Jewels. When I first went there he showed me some of his hidden treasures, and some of the huge diamonds and rubies and other precious stones, which he carried, wrapped in thin paper, in his two vest pockets, as most jewellers do.

He gave me a book of memories which was called, "*Visions and Jewels*", which he had published in Yiddish and had it translated into English. It was a book of memories in which he told about his amazing career from a little watch-maker and mender from a small town in Poland to a Jeweller, where Royalty – and particularly Queen Mary – were his customers and the international moneyed high aristocracy, including Hollywood Stars. But of all of these his most honoured customer (and of whom he was the most proud) was Queen Mary. They usually telephoned from the Palace that she intends to pay a visit to his shop, and he would wait for her, shut up his shop at Cameo Corner to all other customers, and nobody would be able to get in.

Queen Mary, he told me, liked bargains and bought all her Christmas presents in his shop. And very often he would sell pieces of antique jewellery to her below cost price. I always knew that he was expecting a visit from her when I saw, on an ordinary week-day, the curtains drawn, and a sign "Closed" on the door.

One day, he told me, that he was called to Buckingham Palace with some samples of his choice jewellery. He took with him some of the best pieces he had in his collection. He went out and hailed a taxi in the street, and ordered the driver to take him to Buckingham Palace. The driver, looking at his prospective fare, took the address as the standard Cockney joke: "Where did you say? Buckingham Palace? Look here, Guv, I have no time for your jokes! Tell me where you want to go ... or get out of my cab!"

In defence of the cab-driver I must say that one couldn't blame him much, because Moshe Oved, in his own design of clothes, a purple velvet tunic, without buttons, a long black coat with wide sleeves, and a huge soft, black Rembrandt hat on his Albert Einstein head, did *not* make him look like someone used to visiting Buckingham Palace!

He had to give the driver his fare in advance in order to convince him that he was not a lunatic or a prankster, but a legitimate passenger going exactly where he had said he was.

He told me an interesting story about Queen Mary, for whom the British people had a special love, and wherever she visited his shop, even when the black Royal Bentley did not stop directly outside the shop at the corner of New Oxford Street, there always gathered outside a crowd of people waiting to have a glance of her and cheer her, and some even greeted her with loud cries: "Long live the Queen!" Her Majesty was immensely gratified by such a spontaneous show of loyalty and love. But, one afternoon she arrived at the Cameo Corner, made her purchase of little pieces of jewellery for Christmas presents, when she left the shop there was no crowd outside to greet her ... not a soul! The Queen could hardly hide her disappointment at the absence of her loyal subjects to greet her, and Moshe Oved was desperate at the sudden apparent fall of her popularity. When this melancholy scene of nobody waiting to cheer her repeated itself on a second occasion, he decided to find out the reason why, and within a few hours he discovered the cause: At the corner of his shop was an old newspaper man who sold his evening newspapers in the streets. He, it turned out, had always told his regular customers the good news that the Queen is inside Cameo Corner doing her shopping, and they naturally all waited for her to come out, because who in England would miss a chance at getting a glimpse at the Royal family, let alone the Queen herself, if they could actually see them in the flesh?

But, as Moshe Oved soon found out, the old newspaperman had died, and there was nobody there any more to gather the crowds and tell the passers-by the cheerful news.

Moshe Oved also played a decisive part in my possibility of keeping hunger away during the first months of my sojourn in London. My only income was from the articles or short stories that I wrote for the *Jewish Post*, for which I was paid £1. for a piece.

It is true that rent and food I had free in the Jewish Shelter, where I was a privileged guest, not having to sleep in the general dormitory with other immigrants, or eat in the communal dining-room.

I had a large room to myself on the second floor, and took my meals with the Directors family, the Michalsons, who were particularly nice to me and very kind. I was only afraid that they had an eye on me with regard to their daughter, a fat, unprepossessing girl of about my age. And I decided to escape from this free home and look for a room for myself. I went around looking for cheap lodgings in Fitzroy Square, where I knew that at number One, once lived Bernard Shaw; but the landlady who opened the door was a ghastly, blowsy, creature, that I decided better to sacrifice the possibility of being inspired by the wit of G.B.S., whom I greatly admired in those days, than have such a monstrous drunken landlady. In any case the house and the room, dark, dismal and smelling of old rot, was too awful even for me … so I thanked her for showing it to me and left.

I wandered around Holland Street and remembered that I had read somewhere that Verlain lived there with Rimbaud, but I couldn't find the house. Looking around there I saw a blue plaque on a house which said Constable lived there. There was also a sign "To Let" in the window. I went in and found it so filthy that I didn't even dare look at the room which was vacant!

After walking the streets for hours, I finally found a room in a little house on Fitzroy Street, just off the Square. The rent was five shillings weekly, which was quite a handsome sum for me in those days. There was a gas metre where I put in pennies.

Though I had seen nothing cheaper in this half-slummy district, it was at least near the British Museum. Moshe Oved came to the rescue by offering me a light job of secretarial work which consisted of typing his manuscripts and correcting, as much as I could, his mistakes. Unfortunately his poems were bad William Blake in Yiddish, and I prayed to Heaven that he would write something good, because I liked him for his peculiar originality and marvellous sense of Jewish humour. His Yiddish poems, in a folkloristic vein, were sometimes quite good and even original.

Mose Oved paid me the handsome salary of three pounds a week, and when he felt generous he would push into my hand a white fiver. He also gave me a letter of recommendation to the British Museum public Library, and I got a reader-student's ticket which entitled me to see the greatest treasures of the greatest library in the World, and it's rare manuscripts. A recommendation from Moshe Oved meant something in the British Museum. He was a persona grata with it's director for the many presentations he made of ancient Greek and Roman jewellery and Oriental, and in particular, Chinese and Japanese ivory carvings and *netsukes* of which he had the best collection in London.

It was, therefore, a happy day for me when I was given a personal Reader's ticket, which opened for me the treasures of the greatest world library with some seven million books and manuscripts, which became my home for the next six to seven years. I must have spent more time in the Museum Reading room than in my own room. I used to go there just after nine o'clock in the morning, when they opened, and I was there reading until just before six, when they closed, with a few breaks for a cigarette on the front steps or on the benches. I would also go for lunch to the Express Dairy round the corner, where I usually had two rolls with one pat of butter, or if I was affluent, I had a standard steak and kidney pudding or something similar, with one of their famous English sweets, a "Diplomat" or a "Princess" pudding, which I enjoyed. When I was "rolling in money" I went, after six o'clock, to the popular cheap Italian restaurant of Bertorelli in Charlotte Street, where one could have a good meal with a sweet for two shillings and sixpence – including black coffee.

There were days when I was penniless and I had to borrow half-a-crown from an acquaintance in the Reading Room. On one occasion, when I was hungry and couldn't even go for tea in the basement restaurant of the Museum, I was sitting on a bench outside when I noticed that a pigeon had just laid an egg on the stairs – as if I was another Elijah, I went down and opened the tiny egg, with its thin shell, and swallowed it in one gulp!

But, I haven't told you yet what I did with my first pound which I had earned from the *Jewish Post*. I wouldn't mind betting you that you'll never guess!

When I walked out with my single pound, I had in my pocket one solitary shilling, and the first thing I did was to march in to a Dunn Hat shop – and I bought myself a Bowler Hat, the price of which was one guinea – just the amount I had in the world. I had to walk back to the Museum.

I celebrated my Englishness with that black head-gear, without which I couldn't imagine a true Englishman.

And, in honour of Charlie Chaplin, I bought later a walking stick. It was a long time after this that I had the courage to buy a brown Bowler hat, which I had made for me at one of the best hatters in London. To complete my English attire, I later bought an umbrella and a Burberry, and, of course, a Dunhill pipe. I was a passionate cigarette smoker, and I didn't know then that it will take me more than thirty years to learn how to smoke a pipe, although I had tried around the World every tobacco from the best to the worst. I very soon found out that England produced the best pipe tobacco in the world and that all the others are bad imitations, with the exception of some American tobaccos. Not only was I a passionate smoker from my fourteenth year onwards, but I studied diligently the history of smoking and who of the great men were smokers. I was pleased to find that Spinoza smoked his Dutch clay pipe in the evenings. And I was delighted to read that it was the Jewish translator, Lopez, on Columbus's first journey (who many historians now believe was a Morano Jew) was the one to bring back to Spain the "Heavenly Weed", tobacco, which was the inspiration of so many poets, writers, artists and scientists. That this ravishing Lady Nicotine would also ravish the lungs of so many, was unheard of in those days.

I read voraciously, having sometimes as many as twenty to thirty books brought to me on my desk. Often I tried to imagine whether

Marx or Lenin, Engels or Bernard Shaw had sat on my big, not very comfortable, hard chair suitable for the largest scholarly behind.

One day I decided once and for all to read, or at least to hold in my hands, a Folio of Shakespeare, of which there are only five or six copies left in the world. When the Library clerk brought me the Folio I looked through it greedily, and felt as exalted as Keats on looking for the first time into Chapman's Homer. And I regretted that I couldn't write such a beautiful poem. But imagine my surprise when I came to the "Merchant of Venice", and saw it classified on the title page as – "a Comedy"? Surely *The Merchant of Venice*, which I had read in a translation, is not a comedy but a tragedy? And now I had discovered the biggest misprint in a Shakespeare Folio! I couldn't believe my own eyes. I immediately ran to the large shelves which run round the circular hall where the classics, encyclopaedias, dictionaries and various reference books, together with variorum editions of Shakespeare and other classics, to see whether I am not, by any chance, mistaken.

But, lo and behold, the Comedies, Histories and Tragedies of Shakespeare calls the Merchant of Venice a *Comedy*! The astonishment at my mistake was even a greater disappointment to me than that Shakespeare could have classed this tragedy as a Comedy. If he had at least have called it a tragedy, that a Christian forced Shylock into appearing as a monster. I always hated this play since I read it and saw it played on the English stage. It is a most contrived, false, and stupid play. Shakespeare never met a Jew in his life. There were no Jews in England in his time. But, being a genius, he forgot his stupidity and wrote the sublime lines: "Hath not a Jew eyes? Hath not a Jew Hands, organs, dimensions, senses, affections, passions? Fed with the same food, hurt with the same weapons, subject to the same diseases, healed by the same means, warmed and cooled by the same winter and summer, as a Christian is? ......"

Unlike Marlow, who wrote even a worse bloodthirsty "*Jew of Malta*". Besides, there never could have been such a Jewish money-lender as Shylock in Venice, for the simple reason that the Jewish community of Venice would have excommunicated him or stoned him for desecrating the name of the Jewish People. Moreover, as an

Anglo-Jewish historian, Cecil Roth, has discovered from an old Italian Chronicle, from which Shakespeare took the story – but changed it completely, it was *not* the Jew but a Christian money-lender who insisted on his pound of flesh – from a Jew!

Shortly afterwards, I remember, I was working as an historical advisor on an eighteenth-century film of Lion Feuchtwanger's "*Jew Suss*", with Conrad Veidt and a number of famous English actors and Hollywood stars. I told one of them how perplexed I was by Shakespeare's *Merchant of Venice* when I first noticed that it's a Comedy, and I asked him to explain to me what is a Comedy and what is a tragedy? With Shakespeare, he said with a straight face, if a play ends without a number of corpses lying around the stage – *THAT* is a comedy!

Soon afterwards a tragic incident happened to me, which I thought would be the end of my days in the British Museum Library … if not in England. I had a stupid habit of taking with me a library book when I went outside to smoke a cigarette on the steps or porch, continuing my reading while I smoked. On one or two occasions I event went so far as to take the book, quite openly under my arm, across the street to the Express Dairy, where I usually had tea.

One afternoon as I was leaning against a column and sitting on the big steps reading a library book, one of the Library assistants passed by me and noticed the book. "Is this a book from our Library?" he asked me, and took the book out of my hands. "Yes," I said, "I was rather pressed for time to finish it, so I brought it out with me." "I'm afraid," answered the young man, "that I'll have to ask you to come in with me."

He went straight to the Keeper of the Library and told him the whole story of how he found me with a Library book on the steps outside. The Director, whose name was Evans, asked me to give him my Library card, which I did, and told me that I have done something which is absolutely forbidden. He will have to keep my card and that he will let me know tomorrow whether I can use the Library again or not. I think I managed to tell Mr. Evans that I appreciate and value the Library too much not to take great care of the books that are lent to me. And that I really didn't know that one doesn't take out a book even on to the steps of the Museum building. I didn't know whether he believed me, and I went home feeling as if my whole world had collapsed. The end of my studies in the glorious British Museum Library has fallen upon me, and I imagined that this is the end of my days in London … the end of my dream!

How I survived that night, imagining all sorts of misfortunes that might befall me, including being expelled from England back to Poland, I shall never know!

Early in the morning, soon after 9 o'clock a.m., I went in to see Mr. Evans, and imagine my surprise and astonishment and belief when he handed me back my Reader's ticket, with the words: "I hope you wont do this again."

I somehow managed to thank him and went back to a vacant seat. But in my mind I made a vow that if ever I became a rich man, I shall endow the British Museum Library with a couple of hundred new comfortable chairs, and if I find the manuscript of *Hamlet* somewhere in Britain (a favourite phantasy or recurrent day dream of mine in those days), I shall bequeath it to the Manuscript Collection.

Shortly afterwards I had a pleasant and honorific experience in connection with my work as the historical adviser to the film of *Jew Suss*, which Lothar Mendes, one of the first artistic film directors of Germany, was directing. I loved this job more than any other I ever had before. Not only for the glory of working in films, an art which I loved greatly and which gave me the illusion of working with stars of the Hollywood Dream Factories, like Loretta Young and Conrad Veidt, whom I admired hugely (he was one of the great actors of the time), but for the simple fact that I was paid lavishly – £25 per week for three weeks, and, thereafter, £5 a day, whenever I was called. A fantastic fortune and riches for me in those days, when I was paid only £1 per article weekly from the newspaper. And, what's more, I arrived daily in Lothar Mendes's Rolls Royce, which took us from his Mayfair apartment to the Studio in Shepherd's Bush of Gaumount British. The Commissioner in uniform at the gate began to look at me as a rising film director.

Actually my position was a very lowly one: I was to look after the correct costumes of the eighteenth century, and in particularly, of the dresses and hats of the Jews with their yellow badges of the Ghetto on their breasts, and the ceremonies of the Synagogues and the religious schools, the Cheder – in a word, I was to advise and look out for the correctness and authenticity of the period.

One day something very funny happened. I was, on that occasion, away from the Studio and the Producer, Mr. Samuel who, I suspected, doubted my authority, had sent a couple of assistants to the British Museum to make sure about a certain point from the highest Authority in the country, and they approached Mr. Evans, the Keeper of the Museum Library, with the query. Mr. Evans, the same man who had taken away my Reader's Ticket and returned it the next day, who was a great bibliographer, advised them to consult a young man, "who is daily in the Library, by the name of Mr. Honig, who is very familiar with the period!"

They were flabbergasted by this reply, and told him that Mr. Honig *is* already their adviser. "Then you can't have a better man," he said, and bid them good day!

The assistants came back with this verdict to Mr. Samuel, and a day or two later I was shown a cutting of this story in the tabloid *Daily Sketch* (or was it *The Daily Mirror?*) which the Studio publicity department was quick to plant in the Press … to show what kind of experts the Studio employs for this spectacular film, and that nothing but the best will do, no matter what it costs! Needless to say that I went up in their estimation greatly, and Mr. Mendes, the Director, presented me with one of his expensive cigars!

Chapter Twenty-one

My riches, alas, soon came to an end.

The film was finished and my work as historical adviser on the eighteenth-century Jewish life was no longer needed, but Lion Feuchtwanger, the author of "Jew Suss", came to my rescue. I had met him two or three years before when he came to London. It was in the summer of 1932. He had just published his last work in Germany, "*Der Yudische Krieg*", translated into English as "*Josephus*", which I read immediately, and asked him, when I went to see him in the exclusive Connaught Hotel, to give me the rights to translate it into Yiddish.

Feuchtwanger, a small, bespectacled man, with a lined pale face, like an old lemon, was, apparently, pleased with me and my visit although, as he told me, he was waiting for some important visitors, Sir (later Lord) Herbert Samuel, the former controversial High Commissioner of Palestine, and some other people. He told me that I am the first journalist who has actually read his works, and added that in Berlin he had a woman interviewer who started with the question: "What books have you written?"

It was a pleasant and desultory talk, jumping from one subject to another, mostly about Germany. I remember him telling me that he received daily dozens of letters and threatening telephone calls, that they will hang him on the nearest lamp-post when the day will soon come! Feuchtwanger had the high distinction of being the most hated German Jewish writer. Hasn't he written a most prophetic novel about the proto Nazis and what they will do when they'll come to power? That remarkable novel was *Erfolg*, (Success), which had not then been translated into English. It was about a year before Hitler came to power and, I remember, pleading with him not to return to Germany, as he intended to do. His reply was characteristic of him: "But I'm a German writer, and I must hear the German language!"

Feuchtwanger, however, went to America, and when I saw him on his return, he informed me how he first heard that Hitler took over power in Germany.

It was in the middle of a reception which the German Embassy in Washington gave for him on his arrival there. During dinner the Ambassador was called away with a special message by one of the Secretaries. When he came back, after a short while, he took Feuchtwanger into his office and told him … "Adolf Hitler has been made Chancellor!"

However, he didn't return to Germany but went to France and stayed there, where he was arrested just before the outbreak of the War, kept in a Concentration camp for "… suspect German Agents" (mostly famous anti-Nazis), and with the help of his wife Martha, he escaped, dressed as a peasant woman, and was smuggled over the border into Spain.

I was working on the translation of Feuchtwanger's "*Josephus*" and I managed to sell the serialisation rights to the only Yiddish newspaper left in London, the *Jewish Times*, and also to Buenos Aires, where the serial appeared for about a year.

I never translated anything with greater pleasure. I even managed to sell the manuscript to a publisher in London, for which he paid me very poorly – and he thought it too risky to publish it in book form. London has long ago ceased to be a City that could publish a Yiddish book.

★

To write an autobiography one sits in judgement upon oneself.

But can one be a true judge of oneself? Isn't one inclined to be lenient and sometimes too severe?

Think of the "terrible" sins of St. Augustine. He stole in his childhood apples, for which he goes on to beg God to forgive him.

But he hardly mentions the bastard son and the mistress whom he forsook after eight years … . Think of Rousseau, who doesn't mention the children he put into a Foundling Home and never saw again, and started writing books on how properly to bring up and educate children …

There are even historians who believe that Rousseau didn't write the whole truth about himself. But is it possible to write the whole truth about oneself?

Socrates, they say, often repeated the famous words: "Know Thyself." But did he know himself as his poor Xantippe knew him? And Goethe said: "Know Thyself? If I would know myself I would run miles away from me …"

I try to write the truth, more or less about myself as I saw myself. I thought, for instance, that I am not a bad man, and I couldn't discover in myself great evil. But I wasn't that good either. My selfishness wasn't mean, although I certainly was egotistical, but not to harm anybody.

I wanted to be praised, and when I was young I wanted to be famous, because if I'll be famous I shall not be starving. The fear of starvation, of hunger, was uppermost in my mind, having read so much about the poverty of famous men when they were young.

Another thing, besides starvation, that I was frightened of was graphomania and syphilis. Hence my horror of prostitutes, and my fear of writing too much.

I wrote very little, excepting bread and butter articles and journalism.

It was about a year and a half of my arriving in London, where I was lonely and friendless, that I was to meet the girl who was destined to become my wife and the mother of my children.

Perhaps the way I met my future wife is not uninteresting and worth the telling.

I was walking one evening along the Strand when I bumped into a man whom I knew slightly, a singer. Suddenly he said, "I shall introduce you to a nice English family, the husband is a pianist and comes also from Poland. You ought to meet them … and you could always get a decent meal there. You'll like them. Come on, I'll take you there now. They live in St. John's Wood, and we can take a 13 Bus."

I readily agreed, and we took the next bus, which dropped us at the corner of Finchley Road and Boundary Road.

When we entered the house I was pleasantly surprised by a very tall, very elegant woman of a beauty that only English women seem to possess.

After some trivial small talk I said to her, by way of paying her a compliment, which was more genuine that I thought: "If you have a sister, as beautiful as you, I'll marry her!"

To my astonishment she said that she has, and that she will be here on Saturday evening when I can meet her. It will also be the sixth birthday of her little girl, Xenia, and there will be a little party to celebrate.

That question and her answer had sealed my fate!

The next Saturday I presented myself at the Finchley Road house, and was taken up to the music room where there was a grand piano. Her husband, Benio, a talented pianist and a good and witty man (who was later to become my closest London friend) was at home and welcomed me. His wife, Sheila, was preparing for the birthday party of their young daughter.

Half an hour later, as I was sitting by the gas fire, a young woman, with auburn hair and a perfect complexion, entered the room and introduced herself: "I am Pat, Sheila's sister …"

I've been stuck with this sentence for about a week. I couldn't go on. As if, by some mysterious psychological block.

I am writing about a young woman who was destined to change and guard my life for over forty years. There are only two miracles that saved my life: One was coming to England and remaining in London, and the other was meeting this young woman of twenty years old.

I always thought that I was born twice: Once in Tomaszow, Poland,

and the second time in London. I didn't know then that England will become my Mother-in-Law, just as I didn't know that Pat will become my wife, and England – not my step-mother, as Poland had been, but my good mother-in-law.

One is self-conscious to say nice things about one's wife, particularly in England, just as one cannot praise England. It's considered "bad form", when you make a compliment to an Englishman. He may secretly be pleased, but he will never admit it. Try and tell an Englishman that England is a wonderful country, a unique country in its civilized humanity, and he will be embarrassed, he'll feel uncomfortable or he wont believe you. In England I learnt very early that you mustn't praise England ... unless it is in the company of foreigners.

You can say to an Englishman that England (and when we say England we generally mean the whole of Britain) isn't a bad country at all; there is something to be said for England. You can even say, as that unconscious wit (or was he only *too* conscious?) has said: "English humour is not to be laughed at…"

I was an early Anglophile, but I tried not to say it. I have lectured all over the world practically, but I found it only difficult to talk about England to British people in England. We shall have occasion to return to that subject as we come to my lecturing.

My English was still very poor, but I tried to improve it by reading both literature and the daily newspapers for my job as foreign correspondent. I had very little practice in hearing or speaking English, but I went a good deal to the theatre and cinema.

I remember being amazed that so many people, both men and women bought their own papers and read them in the buses and underground, and not, like in Poland, where people borrow the papers from each other. More amazed was I when I saw quite often a newspaper stand, where people took their papers and put in a penny, or two pence for *The Times*, in the box without an attendant.

★

As the writer of these memoirs, Camille Rachmil Honig died suddenly on February 6th. 1977, I, his wife – "Pat, Sheila's sister" – having typed this whole manuscript, can only ask you to look back a page or two where he wrote:

"I've been stuck with this sentence for about a week. I couldn't go on. As if by some mysterious psychological block!"

And so I can only re-title it:

THE *UNFINISHED* WANDERINGS OF

A WONDERING JEW.

(My beloved husband – Camille …)